CW00500826

THE CONSPIRACY FILES

ANNUIT CŒPTIS
MDCCLXXVI
NOVUS ORDO SECLORUM

THE CONSPIRACY FILES

EVIDENCE BEHIND THE WORLD'S MOST NOTORIOUS THEORIES

KENN THOMAS

PIER 9

Published in 2007 in Australia by Pier 9, an imprint of Murdoch Books Pty Limited

Murdoch Books Pty Ltd
Pier 8/9, 23 Hickson Road
Millers Point NSW 2000
Phone: +61 (0)2 8220 2000
Fax: +61 (0)2 8220 2558
www.murdochbooks.com.au

Copyright © 2007 Elwin Street Productions

Conceived and produced by
Elwin Street Limited
144 Liverpool Road
London N1 1LA, UK
www.elwinstreet.com

Design: James Lawrence
Additional text by Joel Levy

All rights reserved. No part of this publication may be reproduced, stored in a retrieval system or transmitted in any form or by any means, electronic, mechanical photocopying, recording or otherwise without prior permission of the publisher.

National Library of Australia Cataloguing-in-Publication Data

Thomas, Kenn.
Conspiracy files: evidence behind the world's most notorious theories.

Includes index.
ISBN 9781921208805 (hbk.).

1. Conspiracies. 2. Secret societies.
I. Title.

909

Printed by Star Standard Industries in 2007.
Printed in Singapore.

Contents

1: Mystery History

2: New World Order

3: Science Faction

Introduction: The Conspiracy Web

The 26 conspiracy files you hold in your hand tell a collective story of mystery and secrets, of disinformation and deliberately jammed circuits. The subjects documented in each folder-chapter range widely—from UFOs to Ancient Egyptians, from mind-controlling governments to gruesomely mutilated livestock appearing, with no explanation, in the cold light of day. But look a little closer, and you might find that the loose threads of unanswered questions—far from being a handful of random strands—could form the beginnings of a web of conspiracy. How were the moon landings, beginning with the first, celebrated one in July 1969, connected with the Freemasons and with the assassination of John F. Kennedy? Is the ancient legend of the Spear of Destiny somehow linked to the rumored Nazi base in Antarctica? These are the sorts of questions conspiracy theorists are trying to answer today, untangling each story strang by curious strand to carefully lay out the web before them.

Whether stuck in a conspiracy web or a spinning one, readers interested in conspiracy material—calling it "theory" deprives it of what makes it compelling, the stubborn facts that contradict the official view—suffer more from schizophrenia than paranoia. Those who openly patronize this extremely popular topic are vilified and accursed by their friends and neighbors, most of whom nevertheless secretly consume the more vulgarized supermarket tabloid form of the genre. The fact of the matter is, the conspiracy web covers the world—a fact demonstrated by the early domination of the World Wide Web by conspiracy theorists. Today, such people are called bloggers. The idea remains the same, however, in the mind of anyone who ruminates on the various possibilities of history and current affairs: it's not crazy to tread warily on the strands of the conspiracy web. It has become, in fact, more enlightening than the mainstream world acknowledges.

Conspiracy theorists run a gamut from serious political dissidents to the actually clinically paranoid. The conspiracy files are showcased at a variety of venues, often undercover, with its cognoscenti disguised as aficionados of something else. They become UFOlogists, alternative media activists, popular culture academics or shoppers at the New Age fairs. Their numbers include bohemians, historians, civic-minded citizens, and victims and wannabe victims of plots. Members from each of these constituencies regularly organize conferences and public events that attract crowds and speakers to examine assassinations, secret political manipulations, and hidden history, often as a corollary to the central topic under discussion. At the Whole Life Expo, a New Age gathering in Chicago, the late psychedelic philosopher Terrence McKenna, for instance, offered his views on the conspiracy to deny an "alien presence" he believed existed on the Internet. Whitley Streiber, the author of a popular alien-abduction book called *Communion*, would have little to do with such a lofty and ill-defined concept, lecturing at the same conference instead on little grey creatures that came to him outside his cabin. Although the two presenters held diametrically opposite views of aliens and spoke to widely different constituencies at the same conference, the two came together on the conspiracy "theory" that mainstream culture deliberately tucks away such possibilities behind a curtain of derision, thus covering them up.

UFO conferences are important in the world of conspiracies. Their underlying assumption—that flying saucers and other unusually shaped space craft frequently visit the Earth and yet remain virtually unacknowledged by mainstream societal institutions—by necessity includes a conspiracy component. The disinterest and outright ridicule of the subject must involve cover-ups by governments around the world. These governments seek to protect the technological secrets gleaned from back-engineering crashed extraterrestrial craft, or claim to protect their citizenry from panic; even worse, perhaps, they disguise their own involvement with alien plots to enslave humanity.

One such conference, the International UFO Congress, meets regularly in the American southwest. While its main program features many of the well-known speakers on the UFO circuit, like David Icke—who presents his own bizarre worldview about shape-shifting reptilians conspiring with world leaders for power dominance throughout history—the lectures that appear further down the program list deal seriously with some quite spooky real-life conspiracy mysteries. At one gathering there was a lecture on the mysterious death list attendant to the UFOlogical community itself. The speaker, Cope Shellhorn, presented a long list of UFO researchers who met their fates in unusual accidents, bizarre murders, suspicious suicides, and fast-acting cancers. According to Shellhorn, "many in this field fail to reach their full four-score."

Is there a conspiracy behind this? Perhaps the UFO researchers on the list went too far investigating and exposing the connection between UFOs and the government, and had to be eliminated. While propositions such as this may be difficult for some to accept, the UFO conventions also provide a public forum for the discussion of indisputably real and mysterious death lists that receive little attention in any other venue. In this marketplace more than any other, people share an excitement of conspiracy talk, begin to trade arcane information, and become inspired to pursue their own research. After the Shellhorn talk, for instance, the focus at one table concerned the list of deaths from the late 1980s involving Star Wars defense contractors. More than a dozen scientists working on the Star Wars defense initiative, SDI, all highly trained technicians on supercomputers and the most advanced military hardware, either could not drive cars well enough to avoid lethal wrecks or were apparently so depressed by their high-paying, high-profile lifestyles that they committed suicide.

Similar mysterious death lists appear in other areas of the conspiracy files, the most recent list involving microbiologists. Specialists in virology, bacteriology, and biowarfare have fallen off bridges, been bludgeoned to death, or, in one case, accidentally locked into a refrigeration chamber. The most noted person on this list is microbiologist David Kelly, the UK Ministry of Defence's chief scientific advisor, found near his home in Southmoor, near Abingdon in Oxfordshire, in July 2003, the victim of an apparent suicide. Kelly's role in the United Nations' investigation of Iraq prior to the war, and his potential as a whistleblower against UK and US intentions there now, made him a ripe cause for conspiracy theorizing.

UFO conferences are more than just a collection of people with fanciful imaginations and tinfoil hats; they draw together common citizens who share normal concerns about the secret machinations of their governments, specifically in the areas of advanced technology and the suppression of civil rights.

Though conferences devoted exclusively to the topic of conspiracy have generally been ancillary to the UFO gatherings, those conferences observing important assassinations have at times turned into large commercial operations. Prominent among them is the Conspiracy Conference, held in the northern California area, near San Jose. Underscoring the importance of questioning rather more Earth-bound events, Conspiracy Con promoter Brian Hall asks, "How can we even begin to address the possibility of life and intelligent civilizations on other worlds if we don't even know who we are and what is happening right under our noses?"

"How can we even begin to address the possibility of life and intelligent civilizations on other worlds if we don't even know who we are and what is happening right under our noses?"

These conventions that concentrate on the role of conspiracy in presidential assassinations were first put on by an activist community that formed over public dissatisfaction with the conclusions of the blue-ribbon Warren Commission concerning JFK. In fact, many of these early conferences looked like amateur Warren Commissions, with participants solemnly delivering their own conclusions on the real individuals, organizations, and political forces behind history's most famous murder. Academic as some of these presentations became, they usually ended in a call for civic action against the government cover-up.

With funding from the wealthy and well-known—including benefactors such as the writer Norman Mailer—the conferences coalesced into what, even today, is known as the JFK research community. In the absence of any real movement to address the wrongs of the Warren Commission, conference-goers became paper tigers, content to refine their conclusions in these specialized conferences for the informed. Oliver Stone's JFK movie bolstered their efforts by renewing attention to this unresolved sore spot in American history. Stone's effort led to the creation of the Assassinations Material Review Board under the first President Bush, and its life was extended under Bill Clinton. The board identified and released many thousands of files pertaining to the assassination that the JFK research community still continues to pore over.

Chief among the current JFK conference organizers is the Coalition on Political Assassinations (COPA), headed by Washington DC conspiracy writer John Judge. Judge works tirelessly both as a classically cast 1960s political activist and as the organizer and promoter of conferences. He sometimes organizes as many as three a year in as many cities, observing the anniversaries not only of JFK but also of Robert F. Kennedy and Martin Luther King in 1968 (in Dallas, Los Angeles, and Memphis, respectively). Driven by the zealous social conscience of John Judge, the COPA conferences appeal to the hardcore researcher with detailed examinations of the medical evidence, and the documentary paper trail of mafia figures and intelligence agencies connected to the JFK hit, and lesser-known celebrities such as the comedian-turned activist Dick Gregory. The COPA conferences now attract both distanced academics and those who clamor for political reform.

The origins of the conspiracy web remain in part in the marginal milieu of small presses devoted to a wide variety of subcultures and specialty interests, including Satanism, Marxism, the Situationists, the anarchists, the nihilists, erotica, and the Reichian orgone, as well as UFOlogy and conspiracy. The most historically well known of such conferences is the 1992 Phenomicon held in Atlanta, Georgia. This brought together a number of young writers who later became big fish in the small conspiracy pond. These included Jim Keith, renowned as the author of a series of conspiracy books, including *Black Helicopters Over America*; Len Bracken, who wrote a comprehensive overview of conspiracy questions related to the 9/11 disasters called *The Shadow Government*; and Adam Parfrey, whose Feral House press has grown today into one of the premier alternative presses in the United States. Such convergences of the literary and artistic bohemian element, although percolating perpetually in coffeehouses and bookstores, do not happen often. One such conference, the Disinfo Con in New York in 2001, became a media event and the subject of a book and DVD documentary. Amid stage shows that included an entourage called the Wall of Vaginas and a performer setting off explosives from his chest, Disinfo included two speakers from the Phenomicon of a decade before: Adam Parfrey; and the perennial conspiracy satirist, *Illuminatus* author Robert Anton Wilson.

If the popularity of conspiracy in the mass media, in such thriller TV shows as *X-Files* and movies like *Conspiracy Theory*, functions as a siphon for a waning credibility of government and mainstream media, what can be said about its emergence among actual people talking to each other about outlandish and not-so-outlandish premises, armed with arcane but nevertheless true facts and with an attitude about civil rights, human liberties, and the paucity of official explanations?

As a part of public discourse, conspiracy talk happens more and more frequently and in a wider variety of forums, from starry-eyed UFOlogists to serious intellectuals. They are bound to the conspiracy web by the same set of questions considered by the current volume: what would any given conspiracy achieve? How did it manifest itself? In what way was it threatening, and to whom? What will it matter if it was found out and more generally known? Why should we care?

Kenn Thomas
PO Box 210553
St. Louis, Missouri

Mystery History

Novelist Thomas Pynchon comments in one of his labyrinthine and paranoid fictions that history contains "more than one life-line back into a past we risk, each day, losing our forbears in forever--not a chain of single links, for one broken link could lose us all--rather a great disorderly tangle of lines..." Nowhere does this become more apparent than when examining the alternative versions of history that conspiracy theories allow.

Atlantis

Mankind "lost" a continent 12,000 years ago—or did it? Called Atlantis, it may have sat in any of a dozen spots found on sea maps of the Atlantic Ocean before a volcano disaster sank it into near oblivion—or so the story goes.

Right: Detail from Raphael's *School of Athens* (c.1510), showing Plato on the left.

Most mainstream historians and scientists say that no such place ever existed, but there are others who continue to speculate on its location. The story of Atlantis originates from the great Greek philosopher Plato. In his treatise, *The Republic,* he envisioned the perfect society. It would include an educated elite who would be able to distinguish clearly between the "only apparent" and the "actual" reality. Arguably, this has become a paradigm for elite, secret, conspiratorial rule. Plato, in fact, may have been saying what conspiracy theorists routinely assert: that commonplace reality and the world of real knowledge and power are two different things.

Fantasy or philosophy?

The first written references to Atlantis appear in two of Plato's dialogues, *Timaeus* and *Critias*, where Socrates's followers respond to his lecture about an idealized "only apparent" society with the story of an actual one, Atlantis. *Critias* relates a story that was first told to his ancestors by ancient Egyptian priests, of a civilization that existed in Atlantis nine millennia previously. It warred with Athens, became decadent and corrupt, and was finally destroyed by the gods. Although it was born out of the Socratic dialogue, the story of Atlantis became a precautionary tale: Man should bow down to the authority of the gods.

According to speculative history, the civilization of Atlantis sat on a continent in the Atlantic Ocean—the continent and ocean both named for Atlas, one of the sons of the sea god, Poseidon. Plato relates at length the civilization's elaborate architecture and its gold

Left: Reconstruction of the Atlantean city based on Plato's description of a series of concentric walls and canals, surrounding a temple to Poseidon on top of a hill at the center.

paean to Poseidon. In fact, he provides such a level of detail, it might indicate that Atlantis is more than an "only apparent" model for the ignoble end that awaits all of mankind's hubris.

"He provides such a level of detail, it might indicate that Atlantis is more than an 'only apparent' model."

Geographic quests for Atlantis

German prehistorian and geologist Otto Muck argued in his book *The Secrets of Atlantis* that, rather than having been struck down by the gods, Atlantis was destroyed sometime between 10,000 and 8000 BCE when a meteorite impacted on the Earth's crust along the mid-Atlantic ridge. According to Muck, the peaks of Atlantis's mountains now form the Azores.

Many historians and scientists claim, however, that no such place as Atlantis ever really existed, and that the sediment of millions of years found at the bottom of the Atlantic Ocean shows little indication of a sunken continent.

Meanwhile, other researchers have taken Plato's history of the ancient world as a cue to uncover long-lost and forgotten cultures that they have identified as other possible locations for Atlantis. For example, there is speculation that the fabled land might have been the Greek island of Crete, the center of Minoan civilization a millennium before Plato, and one with a powerful navy. Scientists theorize that, 15 centuries ago, a powerful volcanic burst from the nearby island of Santorinas may have caused tidal waves strong enough to destroy the coastal cities of Crete. Those who allow for the existence of Atlantis argue that stories of this disaster might provide the actual basis of Plato's reports.

Scientific evidence for the existence of Atlantis

In 1911, the South American explorer Percy Fawcett described to the Royal Geographical Society in London a lost civilization between Bolivia and Brazil that he believed was an Atlantean outpost. His lecture, replete with tales of giant reptile footprints, inspired Sir Conan Doyle, the creator of Sherlock Holmes, to write his novel *The Lost World*, providing the portal by which the fantasy of Atlantis passed into modern popular culture. H. Rider Haggard, author of *King Solomon's Mines*, later provided Percy Fawcett with a stone idol that had been collected from a lost city in Brazil. Believing it to be from Atlantis, Fawcett had the statue in his possession when he disappeared while looking for the legendary civilization in Brazil in 1925.

In May 2001, sonar mapping discovered an undersea land plateau further north from Bolivia, near Cuba, with apparent architectural edifices resembling pyramids and other structures such as roads and buildings. Researchers suggested that this might be Atlantis, or at least a western outpost of the fabled land. The discovery supported previous predictions that Atlantis would be found in Caribbean waters.

In November 2004, an American researcher named Robert Sarmast revealed that sonar scans taken 50 miles (80.5 kilometers) southeast of the Mediterranean island of Cyprus contained imagery of large trenches and walls. "Their location and lengths match exactly the description of the acropolis of Atlantis provided by Plato," Sarmast insisted. Had Sarmast found the "lost continent," the continent that became known as Atlantis, and which had purportedly been submerged 12,000 years earlier into the Atlantic Ocean?

Contemporary coincidence?

Most recently the nexus of interest about the location of Atlantis returned to the land of its origin, at least its literary one. Few expected that Sarmast's discovery would be greeted with any academic curiosity. However, he claims, "We found more than 60 to 70 points that are a perfect match with Plato's detailed description of the general layout of the acropolis hill of Atlantis. The match of the dimensions and the coordinates provided by our sonar with Plato's description are so accurate that, if this is not indeed the acropolis of Atlantis, then this is the world's greatest coincidence."

Sarmast continues to organize further exploratory work to support his theory about the location of Atlantis. Of course, the physical location of the fabled continent answers only a question of geography. From there, the questions about advanced ancient civilization, modern denial, and any academic cover-up of that possibility, remain.

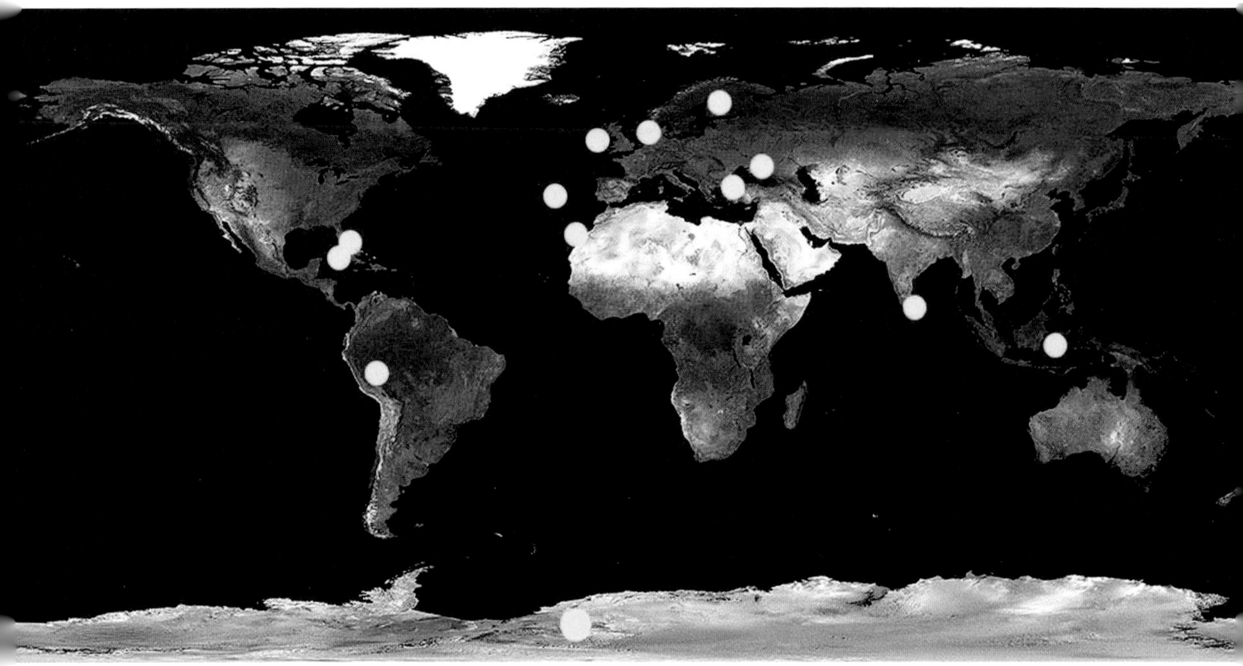

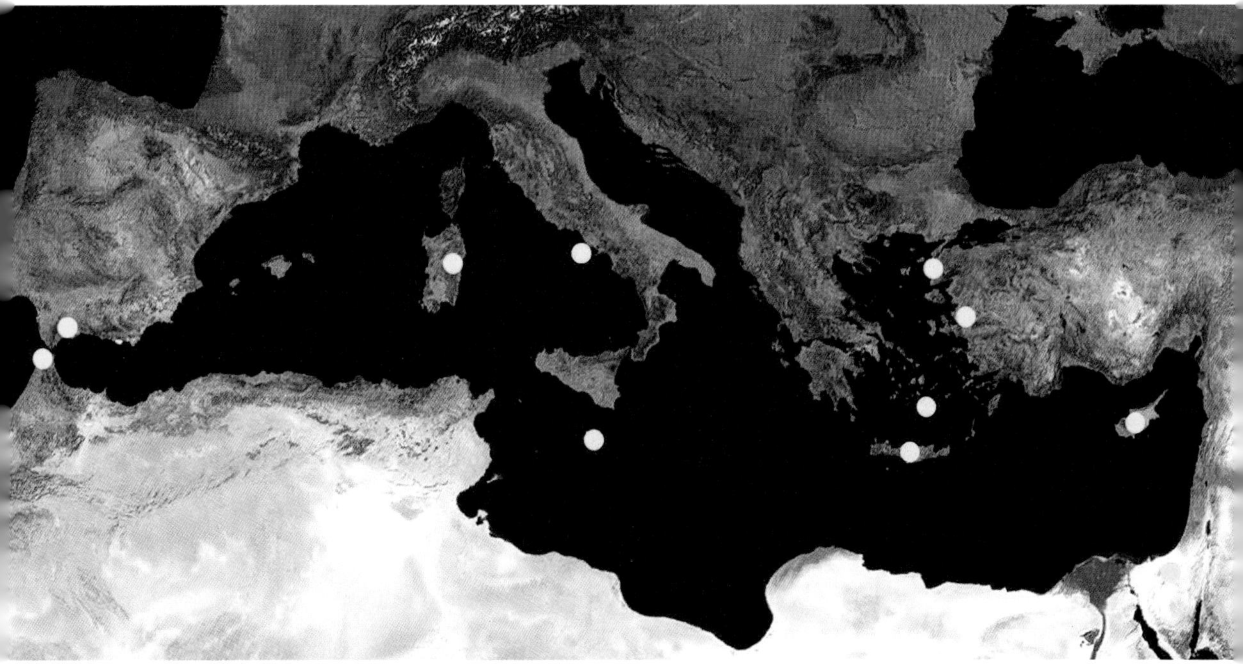

Hypothesized locations for Atlantis, worldwide (*top*) and in the Mediterranean (*above*). Many theories regarding the location of Atlantis focus on the Mediterranean, partly because of the story's origins in Ancient Greece.

Pyramids of Egypt

Who built the pyramids? Is there any evidence of an advanced technological civilization having existed in Ancient Egypt? Are these the symbols of a highly developed, yet lost civilization? Or is it all part of an ancient and far-reaching conspiracy that involves the Freemasons?

Right: The Pyramid of Menkaure, the third and smallest of the pyramids of Giza.

The pyramids of Egypt were first constructed as burial monuments associated with royal solar and stellar cults. Standing 483 feet (147 meters) high, the oldest and largest pyramid, the Great Pyramid, houses enormous 70-ton pieces of granite lifted to a level of 175 feet (53 meters)—a manipulation that would seem to evade the tools and techniques of that era. The Great Pyramid's mathematical measurements also reflect an advanced knowledge of astronomy, and the artifacts it holds—made of quartz, basalt, and diorite as well as granite—suggest production by a technique similar to machine casting.

The world's first Egyptologist, William Flinders Petrie, wrote that the Ancient Egyptians must have used methods and techniques beyond the scope of simple copper tools to construct the wondrous pyramids. Today's researchers, including Christopher Dunn (see box, page 18), continue to question whether it was in fact the Ancient Egyptians who built the pyramids, or if there is any evidence for the existence of a technologically advanced civilization at that time.

Roots of Freemasonry

American historians describe the Freemasons as a fraternity originating in the 1730s and formally refer to them as the Order of Free and Accepted Masons. Seventeen United States' presidents have belonged to the order, and imagery of the pyramids, along with Masonic symbols, famously grace the currency of the USA.

European scholars regard Freemasons as a trade guild dating from medieval times, with connections to fourteenth-century

Above: The Giza Pyramids, Egypt. This complex includes the pyramids of Khfu, Khafre, and Menkaure.

crusaders known as the Knights Templar. The Freemasons themselves trace their history back 5000 years, to the construction of Solomon's Temple and the execution of its architect, Hiram. Hiram was executed for refusing to divulge the secrets of the Order. Did those secrets include the knowledge of an advanced technology used to construct the pyramids? If so, why would he need to suppress such knowledge?

If the origins of Freemasonry can be traced back to an Ancient Egyptian religion, an answer to this question may become apparent: to protect its esoteric knowledge. Priesthoods have a history of maintaining secrets—it could be argued that this is the source of their power. For instance, the Pythagoreans of Ancient Greece worked out the heliocentric nature of the planetary system in the fifth century BCE. Copernicus was on his deathbed in 1543 before he would defy the authority of the Church by challenging its standpoint on an Earth-centered universe and publishing his treatise that indicated the Sun in its correct place.

> "Priesthoods have a history of maintaining secrets it could be argued that this is the source of their power."

So who built the pyramids?

The *Freemasons Manual* states:

"Priests secured the mysteries of their religion from the knowledge of the vulgar or uninitiated by symbols and hieroglyphics, comprehensible alone to those of their Order. The fraternity of Ancient Egypt was denominated by the *Hiero-Laotomi*, or Sacred Builders. They were a select caste and connected with government and the priesthood, whilst the ordinary Masons or articifers were of an inferior caste.... Moses was initiated into the secrets and mysteries of the priestly order when in Egypt."

Dr. Zahi Hawass, director general of the Giza monuments, including the pyramids of Giza, Saqqara, Memphis, Dahshur, Abu Sir, and Bahria Oasis, says otherwise:

"Not a single piece of material culture—not a single object—has been found at Giza that can be interpreted to come from a lost civilization. Instead we find an abundance of tombs, bodies, ancient boats, hieroglyphic inscriptions, pottery, and so on, from the Egyptian culture of the Fourth Dynasty, about 2500 BCE. In archaeology we have no evidence of an advanced civilization prior to 3200 BCE. Theories and speculation about a lost civilization seem to excite people more than the discovery of a culture that we actually find at Giza and elsewhere in Egypt, the culture of an Egyptian of whose existence we are certain. It was a great culture. Why do people need to look for another? As scientists, we keep open minds, but we have to base our ideas about the past on archaeological evidence."

"Theories and speculation about a lost civilization seem to excite people more than the discovery of a culture that we actually find at Giza."

PEOPLE IN PURSUIT:

Christopher Dunn

Suggestions of controversy, cover-ups, and conspiracy regarding prehistoric society exist to crush data that promise to shatter conventional academic thinking, says Christopher Dunn, an engineer and the author of *The Giza Power Plant: Technologies of Ancient Egypt*.

"The opposition by mainstream Egyptologists is like the last gasp of a dying man," Dunn says. "In the face of expert analysis they are striving to protect their cozy tenures by arguing engineering subtleties that make no sense whatever."

Challenging conventional notions about the pyramids, Dunn promotes an undercurrent of speculation that the pyramid builders were highly advanced in their technology. "Attempts to build pyramids using the orthodox methods theorized for the Ancient Egyptians, have fallen pitifully short," he argues.

In August 1984 Dunn published an article in *Analog* magazine entitled "Advanced Machining in Ancient Egypt?," building on ideas set forth in Sir William Flinders Petrie's work from 1883. Since then, he has made several visits to the sites of the pyramids in Egypt and says he has left each time with even more respect for the industry of the ancient pyramid builders–an industry that no longer exists anywhere in the world today. In 1986 Dunn visited the Museum of Egyptian Antiquities in Cairo, Egypt, to give a copy of his article and a business card to the director. "He thanked me kindly, then threw my offering into a drawer with other sundries, and turned away," says Dunn. "But another member of staff in the museum led me to the tool room to educate me in the methods of the ancient masons by showing me a few cases that housed primitive copper tools.

Twentieth-century speculations

In December 1999, the Egyptian government cancelled plans to place a new golden roof on the Great Pyramid to commemorate the millennium. They had originally planned to lower a 30-foot-tall (9.1 meters) cap of gold onto it at the stroke of midnight. No official reason for the cancellation was given, but rumors suggested conspiratorial in-fighting among the authorities in charge of the historic property. Hawass's plans for the ceremony seemed elaborate and, to some, rooted either in the dicta of the ancient Masons or the more modern prophecies of the American psychic Edgar Cayce (1877–1945). Hawass explains:

"One of the reliefs shows workmen dragging a capstone, and there is a statement in hieroglyphs that the capstone was cased in gold. The other relief depicts a scene of ladies dancing. The pyramid's construction was a national project—every household would participate by sending food and workmen to help the king. My interpretation is that when the Ancient Egyptians finished building the pyramid, the king and government officials cased a capstone with gold and placed it on top of the pyramid. This symbolized completion of the pyramid, and everyone in Upper and Lower Egypt danced and sang because the national project of constructing the pyramid was successfully finished."

However, according to Ali Radwan, Professor of Egyptology at Cairo University, the pyramid was built by Khufu, the Egyptian pharaoh from 2589 to 2566 BCE, and not the ancient Masons: "We know that Khufu's father built the first true pyramid. Its capstone was found some years ago by archaeologists and there is no indication that it had a golden surface."

"I asked my host about the cutting of granite, as this was the focus of my article. He explained how a slot was cut in the granite and wooden wedges, soaked with water, were inserted. The wood swelled, creating pressure that split the rock. This still did not explain how copper implements were able to cut granite. I mused that an Egyptologist named Dr. I. E. S. Edwards had once argued that to cut the granite, axes and chisels were made of copper hardened by hammering. This is like saying that to cut an aluminum saucepan they fashioned their knives out of butter!"

Right: Facade of the Museum of Egyptian Antiquities in Cairo.

Christopher Dunn's drill theory

When researcher Christopher Dunn visited the Museum of Egyptian Antiquities in Cairo, he was urged to visit Aswan as well. He was told, he said, that he had to see the quarry marks and the unfinished obelisk there. Dunn arrived at Aswan the following day.

"The Aswan quarries were educational. The obelisk weighs approximately 3000 tons. However, the quarry marks I saw there did not satisfy me as being the only means by which the pyramid builders quarried their rock. Located in the channel, which runs the length of the obelisk, is a large hole drilled into the bedrock, measuring approximately 12 inches (30 centimeters) in diameter and 3 feet (0.9 meters) deep. The hole was drilled at an angle, with the top intruding into the channel space. The ancients must have used drills to remove material from the perimeter of the obelisk, knocked out the webs between the holes and then removed the cusps. While strolling around the Giza Plateau later, I started to question the quarry marks at Aswan even more. I also questioned why the Egyptologist [at the Egyptian Museum] had deemed it necessary to buy a plane ticket to look at them. I was to the south of the second pyramid when I found an abundance of quarry marks of a similar nature. The granite casing stones, which had sheathed the second pyramid, were stripped off and lying around the base in various stages of destruction. Typical of all of the granite stones

worked on were the same quarry marks that I had seen at Aswan earlier in the week."

Dunn concluded that these kinds of quarry marks were from a later time period and were created by people who were only interested in obtaining granite, without caring from where they got it. This discovery confirmed Dunn's suspicion of the validity of Egyptologists' theories on the ancient pyramid builders' quarrying methods. If these quarry marks distinctively identify the people who created the pyramids, why would they engage in such extremely difficult work only to destroy it on completion?

Demonstrations of primitive stonecutting in Egypt are available to all those who visit Egypt. Workers will chip away at the soft, sedimentary limestone blocks to show how easily the stone can be worked. However, Dunn points out: "You won't find any workers plowing through granite! It is an extremely hard, igneous rock made up of feldspar and quartz. Any attempt at creating granite, diorite, and basalt artifacts on the same scale as the ancients, but using primitive methods, would meet with utter and complete failure!"

Many things about the pyramids remain mysterious and hotly debated by Egyptologists. Aside from questions about construction, could a cult of mystical building masons sustain itself in secret throughout history, from ancient Egypt through the American revolution and on until today? Moreover, do they possess an ancient technology still only dimly understood in the modern mainstream?

Left: Illustration of a pyramid being built in Ancient Egypt. Gangs of workers drag blocks of stones up ramps for the next layer.

Jesus Christ

Did Jesus Christ actually exist? Such a question has less to do with belief and faith, and more to do with history and about understanding how such a question might be shaped by conspiracy.

Right: The Turin Shroud (negative view), a holy relic of the Catholic faith.

Below: A nineteenth-century engraving of the Jewish historian Flavius Josephus.

The Catholic Church says of its relics, such as the "True Cross" of the Turin Shroud, that believers should continue to honor in good faith what has been handed down for centuries in good faith. Many Christians would agree that in the end it is faith alone that sustains them, not historical fact; that proof of the existence of Jesus Christ is not necessary to their religious convictions. Is there, in fact, any evidence that Jesus Christ was an actual historical figure? Or is he simply a mythical construct based loosely on events of the time period, whose image has been sustained by the traditions of Christianity and Church authority?

Philo of Alexandria, a Jewish historian who lived at the same time that Jesus was supposedly alive (30 BCE–54 CE), wrote not one word about Christ. Fifty of his voluminous works have survived. Similarly, the Roman historian Livy (59 BCE–17 CE) contributed a detailed account of life under Emperor Augustus without once mentioning Jesus Christ; nor does Plutarch, a Roman biographer, ever mention Jesus. Justice of Tiberius, who authored two important classics, *History of the Wars for Jewish Independence* and *Chronicles: Moses to*

Agrippa, and reported upon the important events between years 30 BCE and 100 CE, does not mention Christ. In fact, Christ seems not to have had sufficient impact to be reflected in any of over 40 extant chronicles of the first and second centuries.

One possible exception is another Jewish historian named Flavius Josephus, living from 37 to 100 CE, whose best-known work, *Antiquities of the Jews*, contains a passage known as the *Testimonium Flavianum*, which is often quoted in defense of the existence of Jesus. It reads: "At this time (30 CE), there lived Jesus, a man full of wisdom, if indeed one may call Him a man. He was a doer of incredible things, and the teacher of such as gladly received the truth. He thus attracted to himself many Jews and many of the Gentiles. He was the Christ. On the accusation of the leading men of our people, Pilate condemned Him crucified him to death upon the cross; nevertheless those who had previously loved Him still remained faithful to Him. For on the third day He again appeared to them as living, just as, in addition to a thousand other marvelous things, prophets sent by God had foretold. And to the present day the race of those who call themselves Christians after Him has not ceased."

"The only record of Jesus in an otherwise mysterious series of omissions from history leads to the suggestion of a conspiracy."

The decidedly Christian character of this excerpt from a Jewish historian's work is the only record of Jesus in an otherwise mysterious series of omissions from history and which leads to the suggestion of a conspiracy.

The earliest known copy of Josephus's *Antiquities* dates from the eighteenth century, a full 1800 years after the (now lost) original. The authenticity of the *Testimonium Flavinium* has been disputed since the seventeenth century, but many modern Christian scholars do now believe that a cleric named Eusebius (c.264–340 CE) forged the Josephus passage about Jesus in the fourth century. Earlier Christian authorities who relied on Josephus's *Antiquities* included such early church fathers as Theophilus, Bishop of Antioch; influential Greek scholar and Christian writer Clement of Alexandria; and Irenaeus, who helped compile the New Testament. Yet Irenaeus made no mention of the passage in *Antiquities* concerning Jesus, which perhaps does suggest that it did not exist in the work at that time, and is indeed a forgery.

These early historians come along, for the most part, two centuries after the life of Christ, as do the Gospel accounts (Luke, 170 CE; Mark, 175 CE; John, 178 CE; and Matthew, 180 CE); the epistles of Paul, however, must have been written before Christ's death (under Emperor Nero in 64 CE). Among them are Tertulian

Right: A torn portion of the Dead Sea Scrolls, one the major archaeological finds of the twentieth century. The documents were discovered in 1947, concealed within jars in a series of caves above Khirbet Qumran, Israel.

and Justin Matryr, the Roman historians specializing in the eras of Claudius, Anthony, and Julius Caesar, and the chroniclers of the public life of Pontius Pilate. Nevertheless, Tertulian and Justin do not recount that Pilate, as Procurator of Judaea, condemned Christ to crucifixion, although each had full access to the surviving public record of the time.

Tertulian likewise never quotes the *Annals* of Tacitus, a historian born two decades after the crucifixion, despite the support of a passing reference in his depiction of Emperor Nero. The *Annals* read, "The emperor, mightily disturbed by widespread rumors among the citizens that he had personally instigated the burning of Rome (64 CE) for his own entertainment and pleasure, threw the full responsibility for it upon the shoulders of a group of conspirators called Chrestiani." Tacitus adds that the Chrestiani were "Jewish subversives, who were brigands or common workers trying to foment a revolt against the established order in the empire."

The Chrestiani

The Chrestiani were a group of Syrian Gnostics, often suggested as being early Christians. They followed the god Chrestus, whose name adorns the entrance of a second-century Syrian church devoted to the Gnostic Marcion. This has been offered by Acharya S., author of *The Christ Conspiracy*, and others as evidence that "Jesus the Chrestos" traces to a Gnostic (that is, Pagan) god, not a Jewish messiah, and is also not an actual historical figure.

"'Jesus the Chrestos' traces to a Gnostic (that is, Pagan) god, not a Jewish messiah, and is also not an actual historical figure."

Interestingly, Pliny the Younger (c.63–113 CE), a lawyer and natural philosopher of Ancient Rome, affirms the existence of the Chrestiani in a letter to his emperor, Trajan, dated 112 CE (taken from the largest surviving body of his work *Letters (Epistulae)*): "Yesterday again, a fanatical sect of local Jews, known as Crestiani, caused street riots and public disturbances against the established religion and the public order. I had their leaders arrested and interrogated. The culprits confessed to holding meetings at daybreak, with the rising sun, praying and singing hymns to one of their gods they call Chrestos."

Chrestos is referred to again in *Life of Claudius* by Roman historian Suetonius (c.69–140 CE): "The Emperor finally succeeded in driving out of Rome those ornery and trouble-making Jews (49 CE) who held stalls in the market place and were stirred to mischief by a fanatical cult called Crestiani." There is no mention of Chrestos, however, and certainly no reference to Jesus, who in any event was said never to have been in Rome.

A critic of early Christianity named Celsus (180 CE) wrote also of "Jewish and Greek nationals meeting secretly in caves to organize for uprising against the established order," accusing "these Crestiani" of such horrible crimes that an early father named Origen refuted him point by point, despite the lack of any reference from Celsus to Jesus or Chrestos.

Certain scholars believe that reports about the Crestiani may describe a group referred to today as the Essenes. The Essenes formed a communistic Jewish sect of some prominence from 1000 BCE to 80 CE, with a large community possibly settling in Khirbet Qumram in present-day Jordan.

In 1947 a Bedouin goatherd named Muhammed-ad-Dhib found the Dead Sea Scrolls near the ruins of Qumram. The discovery of these Qumram Scrolls—a collection of over 700 writings on papyrus, subsequently authenticated by carbon-14 tests as dating from the beginning of Christianity—promised great insight into the history of religion, if not into the life of Christ himself. However, full translation and dissemination of the Scrolls was stalled for 30 years, perhaps in resistance to a reality becoming more and more acknowledged. Only a handful of the Dead Sea Scrolls have ever been fully translated, and debates continue over whether or not

PEOPLE IN PURSUIT:

Acharya S.

"Get over it. Conspiracies exist. This is a big one." Acharya S. does not mince her words when it comes to conspiracies about Jesus Christ. She wrote *The Christ Conspiracy*, a work hailed both by mainstream scholars and in conspiracy circles for the depth of its research into the parapolitical dynamics of Christian mythology. "In fabricating this character of Jesus Christ, a multinational cabal plagiarized myths and rituals that existed long before the Christian era, for a variety of reasons at various points in time," she asserts. "The Romans, for instance, were able to consolidate various pagan cults to create a powerful monotheistic state religion and ideologically unite their empire."

Acharya once served as a trench master on archaeological excavations in Corinth, Greece, on the site where legend has it that the apostle Paul addressed the Corinthians. She also worked on an archaeological site in the state of Connecticut in the United States, and she taught on the island of Crete. She is fluent in Greek, French, Spanish, Italian, German, and Portuguese, and has read Euripides, Plato and Homer in Ancient Greek, Cicero in Latin, and Chaucer in Middle English; she has brought all of this experience to understand Christianity and its origins in more ancient religions. For instance, she felt compelled to cross-reference the Bible in original Hebrew and Ancient Greek.

"It should not be a controversial thing to say that Jesus Christ does not exist as an actual person in history," she explains. "That's only the first, most obvious point to make when looking at Christianity. Not a single shred of evidence indicates that Jesus was an actual man who walked the earth. He's a myth, like any other found in any other religion." She does not make this last point dismissively. In fact, it provides the launch point for a great deal of her writing.

they document the Essenes or another group, the Zealots. Ultimately scholars found that the Scrolls were also devoid of any mention of Jesus.

"Ultimately scholars found that the Scrolls were also devoid of any mention of Jesus."

Belief about Jesus looms largely in the personal philosophy of millions. In many ways, religions often blame each other as being conspiracies against their competing versions of a "true" belief in God. Although many Christian churches offer messages that stress a common heritage, a review of the available research into that heritage suggests that it has less to do with historical facts than many of them assume.

"Most characters in religious mythology, including Christianity, personify celestial events, most notably the solar cycle. The setting and the dawning of the sun provide the basis of a nearly ubiquitous resurrection mythos. The Jesus of the Gospels has adventures identical to the tales of savior-gods such as Krishna in India and the Egyptian god Horus. The similarities of these god-men have nothing to do with the actual exploits of real people who just sort of went through the same thing–that's silly! They reflect an ancient core of knowledge that comes from human observations about the celestial bodies and natural forces."

While *The Christ Conspiracy* reviews the evidence for the non-historicity of Christ, Acharya's writing in general traces the similarities between Christianity and ancient religions, and demonstrates how these mythologies have been co-opted and subverted. *Suns of God: Krishna, Buddha and Christ Unveiled*, her 2004 sequel to *The Christ Conspiracy*, focuses more keenly on the common template shared by the three popular gods. "It's the tale of a miraculously born redeemer who overcomes heroic challenges, teaches ethics and morality, performs marvels and wonders, acquires disciples, and is famed far and wide, only to be persecuted, killed and reborn," says the author. "Sound familiar?"

Spear of Destiny

The Spear of Destiny has been sought throughout history for the powers it supposedly bestows. But does the spear really exist, or is it merely legend? And where, among the various relics that are claimed to be the real spear, is its true resting place today?

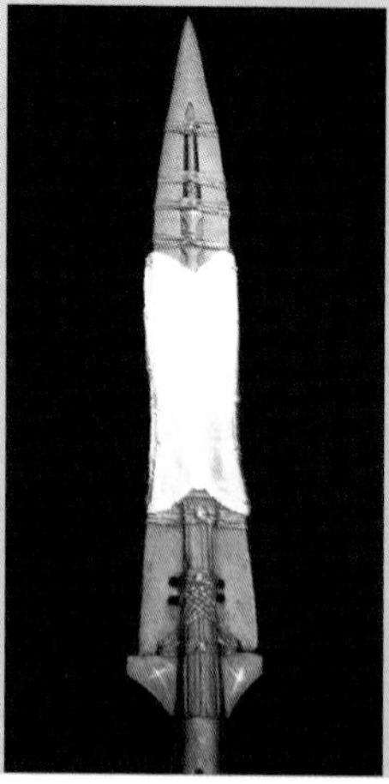

Right: The Holy Lance in Vienna, Austria.

The Spear of Destiny, a legendary weapon from the time of Christ, is purported to confer supernatural abilities on those who possess it, which is why it has been so sought after by leaders such as Hitler. According to legend, the spear took on this magical power after the Roman soldier Longinus used it to pierce the side of the crucified Jesus. Legend also holds that the blood it spilled cured the soldier of his blindness.

The New Testament says only that "when [the soldiers] came to Jesus, and saw that he was already dead, they broke not his legs. But one of the soldiers pierced his side with a spear, and immediately there came out of it blood and water. And he who saw it hath borne testimony of it, and his testimony is true, and he knoweth that he saith true, that you may believe" (John 19:31–37).

"I felt as though... I myself had once claimed it as my talisman of power and held the destiny of the world in my hands."

History of the spear

The name Longinus derives from the Greek word for "spear," and it belonged to another historical figure in Gaius Cassius Longinus, who helped assassinate Julius Caesar, enacting revenge over Caesar for giving Brutus the magistrate position in Syria that had been promised to him.

In any event, the spear represents power, despite a corollary asserting that those who lose it will die. Adolf Hitler coveted the spear. In a dream he saw that the miraculous weapon would aid his plans for world conquest. He wrote of the experience: "I felt as though I myself had held it in my hands before in some earlier century of history—that I myself had once claimed it as my talisman of power and held the destiny of the world in my hands." The provenance of the Spear of Destiny has been traced by researchers through an extraordinary list of owners: Herod the Great, king of Judea (c.74–4 BCE); the Egyptian, Maurice the Manichean, who kept the spear from Emperor Maximian until 300 CE; Roman emperor Constantine the Great, who carried it with him

Below: Longinus pierces the side of Christ. From a fresco by Fra Angelico, an early Italian Renaissance painter.

through great battles and during the building of Constantinople; Theodoric, who put Attila the Hun on the run in 400 years CE; and even Charlemagne, who wielded the spear through many great victories, and died shortly after accidentally dropping it.

Frederick Barbarossa, the Roman emperor of the twelfth century, died when he allowed it to slip into a stream. It passed through several more Roman emperors and German kings until, in the twentieth century, the spear found itself in the hands of Kaiser Wilhelm and eventually became the property of the Hofsburg Treasure House in Vienna. The Hofsburg was where Hitler first possessed it, having conquered Austria on March 12, 1938. He had it brought to St. Catherine's Church in Nuremberg and later secured it in an underground vault. At the end of World War II, the Allies, in the form of General Patton, gained possession of it; Hitler committed suicide, the legend concludes, just after its capture. General Eisenhower ordered the spear to be returned to the Hofsburg Museum, where it remains on display to the public.

The spear in Antarctica

But did the Nazis actually keep hold of the spear at the end of the war? Some conspiracy theorists claim that the original spear

PEOPLE IN PURSUIT:

Jerry E. Smith

Jerry E. Smith is associated with both ends of the history spectrum of conspiracy theories. His best-known book, *HAARP: The Ultimate Weapon of the Conspiracy*, deals with Alaska's High-frequency Active Auroral Research Project (HAARP), a highly futuristic antennae array officially designed to study the ionosphere but suspected by many of being a super weapon. Smith's most recent book, however, explores a weapon from the ancient past. It is entitled *Secrets of the Holy Lance: The Spear of Destiny in History and Legend*.

His interest in the impact of technology on society began at the age of eight, when he read Robert A. Heinlein's *Have Spacesuit, Will Travel*. One of Heinlein's best-known novels for juveniles, it depicts a teenage hero brought into an intergalactic court and forced to defend humanity. Smith absorbed every word and that ravenous appetite extended into an interest in Ancient Greek, Roman, and Norse mythology.

Throughout the late 1960s and early 1970s Smith attended anti-war rallies, worked for liberal candidates, joined the Sierra Club, and formed an intense "Save the World" attitude about environmentalism.

Smith began writing and publishing small literary magazines with his partner Jim Keith, who already possessed a reputation among science fiction fans for his offbeat conspiracy ideas. In 1974 he began to appear regularly in amateur press alliances (APAs) and founded a fantasy fiction club called the Unicorn Society in Klamath Falls, Oregon. Their collaboration was to last many years; during the 1990s, they produced *Dharma Combat*, a magazine of "spirituality, reality, and other conspiracies."

In the early 1990s, on reading Timothy Good's *Above Top Secret*, Smith realized that the study of UFOs always hit upon conspiracy themes. UFOlogy, he found, really concerned itself with captured by the Nazis in Vienna was never actually regained by the Allies. The spear that was recovered was a copy of the original; the real one was transported, along with other treasures plundered by the Nazis, to a secret base in Antarctica. Mysterious tales and conspiracy theories surround Nazi activity in Antarctica, especially regarding the secret development of flying saucers (see pages 116–21). But could the spear really have been taken there? Dr. Howard A. Buechner relates in his books, *Adolf Hitler and the Secrets of the Holy Lance* and *Hitler's Ashes,* how he was contacted by a former German U-boat submariner who claimed to have helped take the spear to Antarctica in 1945. He further claimed to have helped a group of German businessmen, who called themselves the Hartmann Expedition, recover it in 1979, whereupon the spear was taken back to Europe. He provided proof of his claims in the form of the log books of both expeditions. While some conspiracy theorists assert that this was simply an elaborate hoax, others believe it may be partly based on truth; perhaps the true Spear of Destiny really does now lie in a hidden location in Europe after its brief period in the ice.

evidence of government lies and cover-ups. At the same time he read a limited-circulation underground book on the disk-shaped aircraft of Nazi Germany. His attempt to find evidence of the craft and their technical specifications led him to discover that, at that time, a museum of UFOs did not exist anywhere in the world. With Jim Keith, he eventually founded the National UFO Museum (NUFOM) in Reno, Nevada. Smith wrote the NUFOM's quarterly journal, *Notes from the Hangar*.

Smith went on to assemble and write the HAARP book, a compendium of information on a high-tech military facility closely watched by the conspiracy community. "The real question in that book," says Smith, "is how can a democracy defend itself from its own military? I had to ask: what can HAARP do and who would want to do that? Who does that thing really serve? Oddly enough, I came to the same question when I turned my attention to the spear." Smith's *Secrets of the Holy Lance* (co-authored with George Piccard) looks at the many different ideas and stories surrounding the spear's legend, and traces the artifact's provenance from its mythical creation by Tubal-Cain, seventh-generation grandson of Adam, to its appearance at the crucifixion of Jesus Christ; from the Roman emperor Constantine, Rome's first Christian Caesar, to Charlemagne, who claimed that with it he ruled the Holy Roman Empire by divine right; and on through 2000 years of kings, emperors, and rulers up to and including Hitler. "We pursued some interesting questions," says Smith. "Did the spear rest for a while in Antarctic ice? Is it now hidden in Europe, awaiting the next person to claim its power?"

Knights Templar

In modern popular culture, the Knights Templar have become superheroes. But who were they, and what is known about their foundation and influence in medieval history?

Right: Coat of arms of Renaud de Vichiers, the nineteenth grand master of the Knights Templar (1250–1256).

Without the Knights Templar's discovery of the Ark of the Covenant, the sacred container of the stone tablets on which are inscribed the Ten Commandments, director Stephen Spielberg's fantastical *Indiana Jones* movie series may not have been made. Without the Knights Templar's search for the Holy Grail, Dan Brown's novel, *The Da Vinci Code*, may not have had its inspiration. The Knights Templar certainly have a presence in modern popular culture, but what role have they played in our past?

The Knights Templar's rise to power

The Knights Templar was a Christian military order founded in 1118 by a French knight, Hugh de Payens. It began as the Poor Knights of Christ and the Temple of Solomon, following the first Christian Crusade to retake the Holy Land. Its membership included knights and monks, all sworn to keep Christian pilgrims from harm as they journeyed en masse to reconquer Jerusalem after the first crusade of 1096. The name "Templar" is derived from Jerusalem's Temple Mount, the site of the first Jewish temple and the Mosque of Omar, parts of which ostensibly comprised the *Templum Domini*, or living quarters, of the order. Legend has it that the order held the Ark of the Covenant, which contained Aaron's rod and Moses's stone tablets. The residence placed the Knights Templar at the center of the war over the Holy Land. In Jerusalem,

> "The inquisition managed to extract the name 'Baphomet' from the Knights as being the object of worship invoked at their initiation rituals."

and because of their influence in Portugal and Spain, the order accrued vast fortunes and tracts of land.

The order evolved from its soldiering role and in 1128 was recognized by the Church. It grew in power and authority to play a key part in politics and the acquisition of wealth. By 1139 it was entirely exempt from all authority, excepting that of the pope, who gave the knights authority to collect taxes and tithes, as opposed to the local officials. As monarchs and the wealthy elite became the clientele of Templar bankers, their influence both in Europe and Palestine caused suspicion and jealousy from other orders of knighthood.

Above: Al Aqsa Mosque, the first headquarters of the Knights Templar. The Crusaders called it the Temple of Solomon, as it was built on top of the ruins of the original temple.

Friday the thirteenth

On Friday, October 13, 1307, King Philip IV of France (Philip the Fair), arrested and imprisoned Jacques De Molay, the order's grand master, as well as more than a hundred knights. He seized their wealth in order to fund his war against England. This date may be the root of the superstition of Friday the thirteenth. The men were tortured and coerced into confessing to the practice of black magic and occultism; the desecration of the cross; and other heretical behavior, including pagan idolatry. The inquisition managed to extract the name "Baphomet" from the Knights as being the object of worship invoked at their initiation rituals. The Baphomet has been depicted as a goat-headed and two-faced beast adorned with a pentagram—the same demon, according to some latter-day right-wing evangelists such as Jack Chink, as is worshipped by the Freemasons.

Above: Convent of Christ in Castle Tomar, Portugal. Built in 1160 as a stronghold for the Knights Templar, it became the headquarters of the renamed Order of Christ.

Were the tortured prisoners forced into false confessions? Did the Knights Templar actually worship Satan? Recent scholarship, including Baigent, Leigh, and Lincoln's *Holy Blood, Holy Grail*, suggests that the origins of the Knights Templar's rituals and secrecy can be ascribed to an attempt by the order to create a mind-soul split to allow its knights to outwardly perform blasphemous acts, such as denying the cross by spitting on it three times, while inwardly maintaining the faith. This type of duality would have been necessary to the original Templar crusaders who

PEOPLE IN PURSUIT:

David Hatcher Childress

David Hatcher Childress was born in southern France in 1957, grew up in the United States in the mountains of Colorado and Montana, and currently resides in the small Illinois town of Kempton, just south of Chicago. Kempton is the base of Childress's publishing house, Adventures Unlimited Press. It is also the site of an annual conference that showcases conspiracy writers covering themes ranging from the ancient pyramids to modern assassinations, often with an emphasis on Childress's special interest, the Knights Templar.

Childress has spent many years cultivating his understanding of the secrets of the ancient past. His early studies in Asian culture and philosophy at the University of Montana led him on a six-year research and adventure odyssey into the ancient civilizations of Africa, the Middle East, and China. By 1984, he had published two episodic, picaresque books based on his journeys, *Lost Cities of Africa and Arabia* and *Lost Cities of China, Central Asia and India*.

After further expeditions to South America in the 1980s he wrote *Lost Cities and Ancient* were captured and tortured by their enemies. In a similar split, the origins of the demon Baphomet may be found in a mixture of both Christian and Islamic ritual and language. Etymology for the word "baphomet" has pointed to Western interpretations of Islamic vocabulary, "Mahomet" being a medieval Latin rendering of "Muhammed," or "baphonmet" from the Arabic "*abufihamat*," which means "father of understanding."

The *sangreal*

The last grand master of the Knights Templar, Jacques De Molay, was burned at the stake on March 19, 1314, after recanting his confession. His execution marked the end of the Knights Templar. Many in the order fled to Scotland, where, legend has it, they took the *sangreal*, or Holy Grail, and buried it beneath Rosslyn Chapel in the village of Roslin in Midlothian. Others regrouped in Portugal under the name of the Order of Christ and served with distinction in the Portuguese Navy.

Yet some see De Molay's execution as not the end, but the beginning of the secret legacy of the Knights Templar, which has had an impact to this day on world affairs. From his death pyre, De Molay placed a curse on King Philip IV and the reigning pope, Clement V. Clement died the month after De Molay, while Philip the Fair died eight months after receiving the curse; the reigns of his three sons also terminated early. Strangely enough, and perhaps to reverse the curse, according to documents uncovered in the Vatican archives in 2001, Clement pardoned the Knights Templar shortly after De Molay's execution.

The order of the Knights Templar occasionally emerges in the world of secret societies and fraternities. It figures prominently, for instance, in the literature and rituals of Freemasonry, and its name is particularly impressed upon the foundation of the eighteenth-century French Masonic order known as Scottish Rite.

Below: David Hatcher Childress.

Mysteries of South America, which became a bestseller in Brazil. Childress eventually completed an entire series of Lost Cities, which covered ancient Lemuria (the lost continent of the Pacific), North and Central America, Atlantis, ancient Europe and the Mediterranean, and ancient Micronesia.

The revised edition of Charles Addison's *The History of the Knights Templar* (originally published in London in 1842) includes a foreword by Childress, in which he ruminates about the Templar Fleet.

In 1919, the Freemasons started their own form of Boy Scouts entitled the Order of De Molay after the martyred grand master. A charitable organization, the Sovereign Military Order of the Temple of Jerusalem, formed by Napolean and based on Knights Templar traditions, won official status from the United Nations in 2001.

Knights Templar in modern imagination

The Knights Templar continue to capture the popular imagination of enthusiasts in their search for ciphers and codes that unlock history, a confluence that has produced not only *The Da Vinci Code* but an array of titles also inspired by a selection of Knights Templar codes, such as:

Above: Temple Mount, one of the best-known landmarks of Jerusalem, Israel.

- *The Hiram Key* by Christopher Knight and Robert Lomas, which revolves around a secret code to the meaning of events such as the building of the Temple of Solomon, the Egyptian exodus, and the Star of Bethlehem.
- *The Lost Colony of the Templars* by Steven Sora, in which, a century before Columbus, the Templar knight Henry Sinclair encodes the exact measurements of a Templar baptistery in a tower in Newport, Rhode Island.
- *The Templars and the Ark of the Covenant* by Graham Phillip, in which ciphers left by knights in stained-glass windows, church paintings, and inscriptions are traced to ancient gemstones intended to protect the Ark of the Covenant. The author suggests that these gemstones discharge spherical light to disrupt today's electronic equipment.

The various legends of the Knights Templar certainly have some measure of truth, but, more than that, they offer an inspiring and romantic legend. The image of the brave knights with their secret agendas appears in everything from stories of King Arthur and Camelot to the Jedi Knights of George Lucas's *Star Wars* movies. It contrasts greatly with the image of conspiracy mongers as villains and agents for corrupt and evil causes.

POINTS TO PONDER: THE TEMPLAR FLEET

- According to David Hatcher Childress, the Knights Templar had an extensive sea network and were in possession of maps and other secrets of the Phoenicians. When Philip IV outlawed the Knights in 1307, a fleet of ships belonging to the Templar and located in the port of La Rochelle, France, simply vanished.
- Childress believes that, as the exiled Knights fled to areas beyond France, the Templar fleet stopped at the Castle of Almourol, a fortress island in the River Tagus, where they were joined by Portuguese explorers and royalty.
- It is possible that some of the Knights went on to play a role in colonizing Brazil, Portugal's South American territory. "Curiously," says Childress, "Brazil has many Masonic lodges and was originally an independent state established by a wealthy group of Masons who wanted it to be independent of Portugal, in much the same way that Masons and Rosicrucians were instrumental in the creation of the United States. Brazil, like the United States, has deep connections to the Knights Templar."
- Childress notes that Brazil contains a spectrum of cultures, nationalities, and races. Its demographic profile, for instance, includes the highest number of expatriate Japanese of any country and immigrants from all over the world as well as its own Amerindian natives. "Such a racially and culturally mixed nation was apparently the sort of nation that the Knights Templar and later Masons were trying to create," says Childress.
- While Portugal served as a haven for the Knights Templar, southern France and Catalonia (the area of the Cathars and Merovingian kings) provided its main base of operations until the Knights were outlawed.
- This area along the border of Spain and France has long identified itself as a culture separate from the rest of Spain. The people speak their own language, Catalan, which may have originated with ancient Phoenician, while Barcelona, the capital of Catalonia, originally functioned as a Phoenician port and remained an important sea outpost.
- Childress has a further observation on the Knights Templar fleet: "Columbus landed at Barcelona upon his return to Europe from the New World. Why did Columbus come all the way to Barcelona when he had left from Cadiz, a port that he had to pass by on his way to Barcelona? Perhaps Barcelona was a safer port to land at than Cadiz?" Could Columbus have belonged to the Knights Templar? "He always signed his name with curious triangle and coded letters, something which the Knights Templar were known to do." Childress speculates further that, as a sea outpost, Barcelona would have been a more likely city for the residence of the grand master of the Knights Templar.

Rosicrucians

The famous eye-over-the-pyramid symbol featured on the American dollar bill originally belongs not to the Freemasons, as is often claimed, but to a fraternity with even more secret origins: the Rosicrucians. But who are these Rosicrucians?

Right: The Rosicrucian cross, designed by Stanislas de Guaita in 1888.

The Rosicrucians, officially the Order of the Rosy Cross and Ancient Mystical Order Rosae Crucis (AMORC), are a secret society whose seventeenth-century publications announced the arrival of a group of people who were going to transform all aspects of society. However the literary hoaxes and offshoot groups of the nineteenth and twentieth centuries have created a secrecy that makes gathering information on the history, personalities, and publications of the order of adepts virtually impossible. Even its traceable past in the Christian era recedes into an early fog. As with the Masons, who to this day maintain a rank entitled Knight of the Rose Cross, the true beginnings of the Rosicrucians may belong among the mystery religions of Ancient Egypt.

Below: The reverse side of the U.S. one-dollar bill, which features a Rosicrucian symbol, the eye over the pyramid.

Interpreting origins

Rosicrucianism arises from the practice of Gnosticism, a philosophy that stresses inner knowledge and outer secrecy, although many of its ideas also have roots in Pythagoreanism of ancient Greece, Islamic mysticism, and various other mystical traditions. Few people believe that all groups identified as Rosicrucians throughout history can trace a direct line back to the original society. Sources differ regarding the actual origins of the Rosicrucians; some claim it began in 1313, others cite 1407. According to one source, the German founder, Christian Rosenkreuz (1378–1484), originally allowed only eight adepts into the

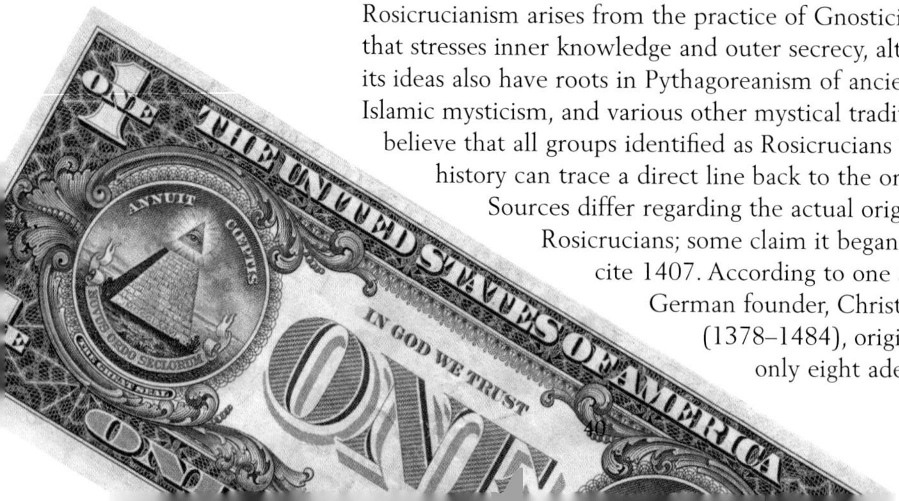

Above: The Jewel of the Rose Croix by J. Augustus Knapp, an illustration from *The Secret Teachings of All Ages: An Encyclopedic Outline of Masonic, Hermetic, Qabbalistic and Rosicrucian Symbolical Philosophy*, the rose and the cross are symbolic of the crucifxion of Jesus Christ and pointing towards the mystery of the Resurrection.

Above: View of the front of AMORC's Rosicrucian Egyptian Museum in San Jose, California.

esoteric group. The order intended to impart to its members the meaning of religious symbols like the rose and the cross, without the cognitive processes of faith or reason. Another version of the story claims that Rosenkreuz continued this teaching only because he had acquired it from Ormus, a Gnostic of Alexandria who had six followers. Ormus was said to have been converted to Christianity by Mark, one of Christ's disciples. Although the two versions are at odds chronologically, both of them include the notion of mystical transference of knowledge about symbols meant to initiate a great change in world religion.

Rosicrucian publications and the conspiracy of authorship

This virtual man-to-man existence, in which a very small group passed down the tradition to another very small group, kept the secret order running until the seventeenth century, when the Rosicrucians published three books: *Fama Fraternitatis Rosae Crucis* (1614), *The Confessio Fraternitatis* (1615), and *The Alchemical Wedding of Christian Rosenkreutz* (1616). This trilogy became popular because of its claim that Rosicrucianism held the secrets of alchemical science and the key to understanding religious symbols. The books, and their many variations and related ephemera, attracted a large audience that looked in vain to find an authentic branch of the group to join. Scholars suggest that a theologian named Johann Valentin Andrea authored the three books simply to popularize his own ideas and interests. Regarded as satire or a hoax by many scholars, the publications are considered by others as providential for the real Rosicrucians, who would have been happy with such clouding of their secrets in the popular imagination.

One motto from Rosicrucian literature of the early 1600s reads: "The thoughts attached to the real desire of the seeker will lead us to him and him to us." In other words, the true Rosicrucian has to be recruited, and attempts to join the order will be in vain. Rosicrucians claim special God-given abilities to heal, which are based on a cultivated spiritual attainment through a unique understanding of astrology by a select few.

"He claimed to have been initiated into the Rosicrucian Order while visiting Europe in 1907, after being taken to a Rose Cross temple."

Max Heindel and the introduction of Rosicrucianism to America

Nevertheless, according to one self-proclaimed descendant group of the Rosicrucian fellowship, an adept named Max Heindel brought the teachings of the Rosicrucians to a wider audience in America in 1908. Born in Aarhus, Denmark, in 1865, Heindel emigrated to the United States, settling in Los Angeles in 1903. He claimed to have been initiated into the Rosicrucian Order while visiting Europe in 1907, after being taken to a Rose Cross temple. On his return to the Unites States, he wrote *The Rosicrucian Cosmo-Conception*, containing the Western Wisdom Teachings, and founded a Rosicrucian Fellowship at Mount Ecclesia in Oceanside, California. The results of his efforts, and those of other members that followed, became noticeable as Rosicrucianism began appearing in popular U.S. magazines, exhorting potential recruits to "Master Your Life" by joining the group via mail order.

Dr. Harvey Spencer Lewis, an American businessman and the former director of the Institute of Psychic Research in New York, established a Rosicrucian Park in San Jose, California, in 1927. Shortly after, his AMORC group opened a Rosicrucian Egyptian Oriental Museum, which displayed artifacts of Egyptian symbolism unique to this American offshoot. It has become a tourist attraction of the example of kitsch culture the artifacts have come to represent.

Below: Display of a mummy at the Rosicrucian Egyptian Oriental Museum.

Freemasons

Could the building trade actually be a secret guild that has been responsible for manipulating the development of Western culture since the days of the Egyptian pharaohs?

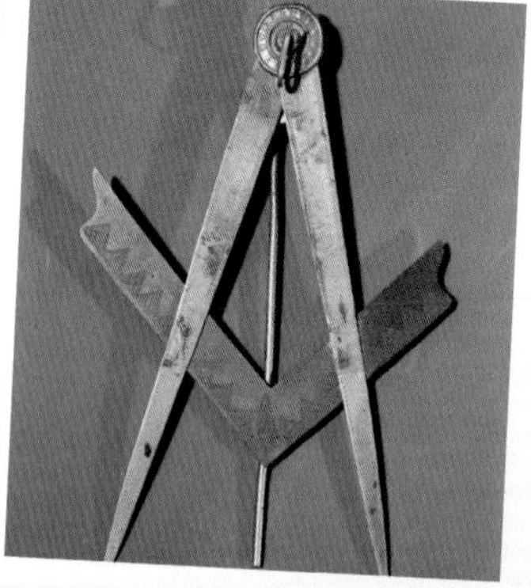

Right: The square and compasses, one of the most prominent symbols of Freemasonry.

That is the question that lies at the heart of speculation about the Freemasons, the most widely known of the world's secret societies. Scholars mainly dismiss the notion that Freemasonry can be tracked as far back in time as ancient Egypt, and most reject that the brotherhood has had a large impact on history. Yet the symbolism of the Great Pyramid appearing prominently on early American currency, and the special handshake shown underneath building-trade tools on the new U.S. nickel, issued in 2004, are undeniable. Symbols such as these arouse curiosity about the place this society occupies in history and the modern world.

In fact, the first American president, George Washington, dedicated the U.S. Capitol building while dressed in a Masonic apron and in 1753 performed a Masonic rite using a silver-plated cornerstone to note the year as the Freemasons record it: "5793."

Hiram I and the roots of Freemasonry

The chronology of Freemasonry begins with Hiram I, king of the ancient Phoenician city, Tyre, and the architect of the Temple of Solomon, the first Jewish temple in Jerusalem. Hiram and Israel's King Solomon presided over the creation of a flat surface on a hill, where the temple was to be built. Their alliance opened trade routes to ancient Egypt for the first time. According to Masonic tradition, Hiram refused to give up the secrets of the guild and was subsequently killed by fellow Masons, as is told in Masonic ritual.

The Ark of the Covenant, containing Moses's Ten Commandment tablets, was brought to the Temple of Solomon by the Knights Templar, another secret group of long-standing affiliation, providing the first connection between the Freemasons and the Knights Templar.

Many great thinkers of the American Revolution belonged, secretly or not so secretly, to the Freemasons. A great split occurred between the Masonic lodges of Britain and the lodges in America, with the issue of colonial independence causing the greatest friction. The Grand Lodge of England subsequently altered many of its secret cues, including the handshake with which members would identify themselves, and they led a breakaway faction known as the Antients. Ironically, the earlier faction became known as the Moderns.

"According to Masonic tradition, Hiram refused to give up the secrets of the guild and was subsequently killed by fellow Masons."

This split makes it difficult to assess the impact of the Freemasons during this period. For example, Benjamin Franklin

Left: George Washington, the first president of the United States, in Masonic dress.

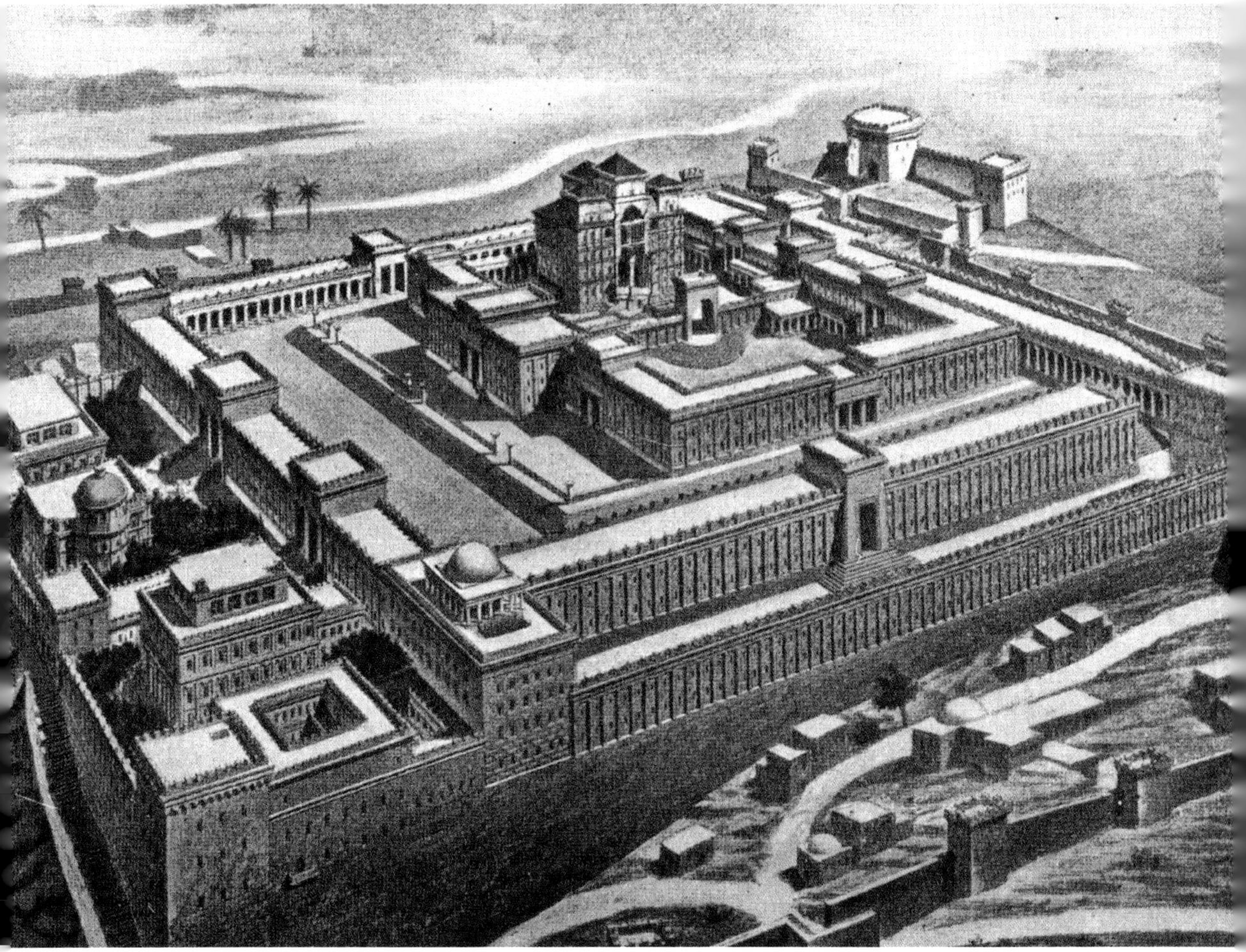

Above: Ideal reconstruction of the Temple of Solomon in Jerusalem, according to the description in the Bible. (This is not a reconstruction based on archaeological grounds).

belonged to the Moderns, but was denied a Masonic burial because his lodge was Antients. Such ideological hair-splitting within a secret society contributes to confusion about the extent of Freemason influence during the revolutionary period.

British impact: Thomas Paine

Despite imprints left by the Masons between Ancient Egypt and the period of the French and American revolutions, most historians look to eighteenth-century Britain when evaluating the group's most profound impact on modern history. This was the time of the Enlightenment, a time of progressive ideas and a rejection of religious authority in favor of authority based on reason. Freemasonry came to embody a liberalism that the conservative mainstream and the Roman Catholic Church associated with being alcohol-driven and licentious. Without revealing the secrets of their society, the Masons had little power to combat this negative image. Pope Clement XII issued an edict in 1738, officially excommunicating all Freemasons. Masonic lodges were regarded throughout Europe as places where radicals planned violent revolutions and, as a result, police raids were frequent and many towns had the group banned from their communities.

It has never been established with certainty that the British-born pamphleteer Thomas Paine, whose 1776 essays *Common Sense* and *The Crisis* convinced many of the importance of America's separation from England, did belong to a lodge. Freemason Benjamin Franklin had advised Paine to move to America in 1774. Paine's concerns included an examination of the ancient roots of guild belief, asserting in an essay entitled *Origin of Freemasonry* that "the Christian religion and Masonry have one and the same common origin: both are derived from the worship of the Sun. The difference between their origins is that the Christian religion is a parody on the worship of the Sun, in which they put a man whom they call Christ in the place of the Sun, and pay him the same adoration which was originally paid to the Sun."

"Masonic lodges were regarded throughout Europe as places where radicals planned for a violent revolution."

After the American Revolution, Paine wrote *The Rights of Man* in support of the French Revolution. He only just escaped imprisonment for inciting rebellion, having fled Britain on the advice of the visionary poet William Blake before he could be arrested. Although he was initially welcomed as a hero in France, he was soon imprisoned there, and barely escaped execution by guillotine after completing *Age of Reason*, in which he described the philosophy of deism that he shared with Benjamin Franklin, George Washington, and Thomas Jefferson.

Freemasonry in America

Freemasonry flourished in America, not openly but as a members-only privilege of the elite and the upwardly mobile classes. It attracted so many wealthy elite that another backlash against the Masons occurred among the electorate in the 1820s with the disappearance of Captain William Morgan. Morgan had just published an exposé on the Masons, *Illustrations from Freemasonry*, when he was abducted and disappeared. The men convicted of the crime were not heavily penalized, triggering outrage that Masonic membership had pervaded the lawmakers and judges to an extent that jeopardized American ideals of freedom and equality. An anti-Masonic political party was formed in 1827, which was the earliest significant third party in American politics. It lost the 1832 presidential campaign to incumbent Andrew Jackson, a Mason. An anti-Masonic campaign was launched by the National Christian Association in 1880 against James Garfield, who won the election, but was assassinated on July 2, 1881.

> "outrage that secret Masonic membership had pervaded the lawmakers and judges to an extent that jeopardized American ideals of freedom and equality"

Freemasons and the Bavarian Illuminati

The impact of the Freemasons on the French Revolution took many forms. The most notable involved a more notorious secret society within it, the Bavarian Illuminati. The head of this group, Adam Weishaupt, joined the Freemasons a year after creating his own secret network, believing it would help to expand his plans to spread the ideals of the Enlightenment and rule the world.

The connection did great damage to the cause, however, when Congregationalist ministers in New England, attempting to strengthen the image of the Federalists headed by John Adams, used it to tar the reputation of the secret guild.

POINTS TO PONDER: U.S. PRESIDENTS

At least 15 U.S. presidents have been documented as holding Freemasonic membership:

- George Washington (the 1st president, 1789–1797)
- James Monroe (the 5th, 1817–1825)
- Andrew Jackson (7th, 1829–1837)
- James Knox Polk (11th, 1845–1849)
- James Buchanan (15th, 1857–1861)
- Andrew Johnson (17th, 1865–1869
- James Abram Garfield (20th, 1881)
- William McKinley (25th, 1897–1901)
- Theodore Roosevelt (26th, 1901–1909)
- William Howard Taft (27th, 1909–1913)
- Warren Gamaliel Harding (29th, 1921–1923)
- Franklin Delano Roosevelt (32nd, 1933–1945)
- Harry S. Truman (33rd, 1945–1951)
- Lyndon Baines Johnson (36th, 1963–1969)
- Gerald R. Ford, Junior (38th, 1974–1977)

Above: The Masonic "clasped hands" symbol on the new U.S. nickel issued in 2004.

Post–World War II anti-Freemason sentiment

Strands of backlash against Freemasonry continued throughout the two world wars and to the present day. Dictators from Franco to Hitler, Mussolini, and Stalin, outlawed, arrested, and executed many Masons. In *Mein Kampf*, Hitler wrote: "The prohibition of Freemasonry and secret societies [...] will enable the Italian government, in the course of some years, to advance more and more the interests of the Italian people."

Today, the secretive nature of the Freemasons is seen by radical Islamic groups as a supporter of the policies of Israel and the United States. The Abu Hafs al-Masri Brigades claimed responsibility for the terrorist bombings in Madrid, Spain, on March 11, 2004. Just two days before this, Jund al-Quds, an allied group, carried out a suicide attack against a Masonic lodge in Istanbul. "America is next," declared the Abu Hafs al-Masri Brigades.

The death of William James the following week, in Patchogue, New York, did much to generate speculation about enemies of Freemasons. The event occurred while he was being inducted at the Southside Masonic Lodge of Suffolk County by fellow member Albert Eid, in a ceremony that was supposed to include firing blank shots to create anxiety, a ritual not sanctioned by Carl Fitje, grand master of the New York State Freemasons.

Contemporary Freemason imagery

The public image of the Freemasons today has become that of a brotherhood, protecting well-intentioned but secularist values via a hierarchical membership structure, secret rituals, symbols, and language. In some respects, it is a secret society out in the open. Its trademark emblem, the builder's square, emblazons car fenders and jewelry, and adorns road signs and lodge halls. Phrases from Freemasonry, such as being "on the square" (the builder's square) and "getting the third degree," have found a place in English language. However, anti-Masonic sentiment continues to pervade some segments of modern society.

> "The public image of the Freemasons today has become that of a brotherhood, protecting well-intentioned but secularist values via a hierarchical membership structure, secret rituals, symbols, and language."

After the terrorist attacks in the United States on September 11, 2001, for instance, the discovery that American $20 bills could be folded in such a way that made the buildings and symbols on the currency resemble smoke rising from the World Trade Center and the Pentagon (see www.allbrevard.net), suggested proof of Masonic/Illuminati foreknowledge of the attacks. The currency of the United States, after all, has encoded Masonic symbols that have provoked debate about their interpretation and meaning in America and the world.

PEOPLE IN PURSUIT:

James Shelby Downard

Of all the writers who have made charges against the Freemasons, James Shelby Downard ranks as one of the most sought out and well known. His thesis is that John F. Kennedy's assassination involved a Masonic ritual to "kill the king" via symbolic manipulation, with its ultimate purpose being to land a man on the moon and further an agenda of earthly domination. "Masonic betrayal of the common man," writes Downard, "involves archetypes of fertility and death symbolism seemingly motivated to bring about syncretism in opposing principles in order to green Israel, rebuild the Temple of Solomon and establish a One World government."

Downard continues: "President Kennedy and his wife left the Temple Houston and were met at midnight by tireless crowds present to cheer the virile 'Sun God' and his dazzlingly erotic wife, the 'Queen of Love and Beauty,' in Fort Worth. On the morning of November 22, they flew to Gate 28 at Love Field, Dallas, Texas. The numerals 28 are one of the correspondences of Solomon in kabbalistic numerology; the Solomonic name assigned to 28 is 'Beale.' On the twenty-eighth degree of latitude in the state of Texas is the site of what was once the giant 'Kennedy ranch.' On the twenty-eighth degree is also Cape Canaveral, from which the moon flight was launched, made possible not only by the president's various feats but by his death as well, for the placing of the Freemasons on the moon could occur only after the killing of the king. The twenty-eighth degree of Templarism is the 'King of the Sun' degree. The president and first lady arrived in Air Force One, code-named 'Angel.'

"The motorcade proceeded from Love Field to Dealey Plaza. Dealey Plaza is the site of the Masonic temple in Dallas (now razed) and there is a marker attesting to this fact in the plaza. Important 'protective' strategy for Dealey Plaza was planned by the New Orleans CIA station whose headquarters was a Masonic temple building. Dallas, Texas, is located 10 miles (16

Above: An American $20 bill folded to resemble smoke rising from the World Trade Center and the Pentagon.

kilometers) north of the thirty-third degree of latitude. The thirty-third degree is the highest in Freemasonry and the founding lodge of the Scottish Rite in America was created in Charleston, South Carolina, exactly on the thirty-third degree line. Dealey Plaza is close to the Trinity River."

Downard also notes several further patterns involving the number three: the Kennedy motorcade went under the Triple Underpass after he was shot; the Trinity River runs near Dallas; and three tramps picked up by police near the grassy knoll have an exact corollary in the three "unworthy craftsmen" of Masonic lore who assassinated Hiram, the architect of the Temple of Solomon.

Downard concludes that "the ultimate purpose of that assassination was not political or economic but sorcerous: for the control of the dreaming mind and the marshaling of its forces is the omnipotent force in this entire scenario of lies, cruelty, and degradation. Something died in the American people on November 22, 1963–call it idealism, innocence, or the quest for moral excellence. It is the transformation of human beings which is the authentic reason and motive for the Kennedy murder and until so-called conspiracy theorists can accept this very real element they will be reduced to so many eccentrics amusing a tiny remnant of dilettantes and hobbyists."

Downard's essay "King Kill 33" has been published in the first edition of the obscure anthology, *Apocalypse Culture*. This goes against the long-standing availability of anti-Masonic writing throughout American history. Subsequent editions of *Apocalypse Culture* include some of Downard's more generalized concepts, but for the most part, interested readers must seek it out on the Internet.

Illuminati

Who were the Illuminati? Were they a heroic driving force behind human progress, or a sinister group, shrouded in conpiracy and consumed by plans for world domination?

Right: The all-seeing-eye, a symbol associated with the Illuminati in modern culture.

The Illuminati—the name covers a number of secret groups and societies—is probably responsible for feeding the imagination of most conspiracy enthusiasts who see the Illuminati stretching back to Ancient Egypt and forward to a New World Order shaped by events such as the terrorist attacks on 9/11. The Illuminati generally refers to the Order of the Illuminati or Bavarian Illuminati; although a secret group decried by its critics for opposing religion and government, it is often championed for being a moving force for secularism and human progress.

Below:
Adam Weishaupt, on eof the founders of the Illuminati.

Founders of the Illuminati

Its founders, Adam Weishaupt, Adolf Knigge, and Xavier Zwack, were instrumental in contributing to the spread of its secret and taboo ideas. Two important writers, John Robison and Augustin Barruél, took the facts of the public lives of these three figures and mixed them with conjecture to transform them into the subjects of conspiracy theories with more far-reaching impact.

Adam Weishaupt officially founded the Order of the Illuminati on May 1, 1776 at the University of Ingolstadt in Bavaria, a southern state in Germany, where he served as a Jesuit professor of canon law. He began the Order in a near-paranoid reaction to his academic status, which he felt had been diminished by the efforts of enemy clerics. As a product of the Enlightenment, Weishaupt favored rationalism over the strict authority of religion, and in a culture dominated by the Catholic Church he found such a disposition—shared by the cognoscenti of the time—best kept secret. The idea of a secret society was highly popular at the time, offering various new modes of behavior, rituals, and beliefs that were a breed apart.

Freemason influences

Weishaupt patterned the Order of the Illuminati after the Freemasons, a secret society well established in the 1700s. He created a three-tiered hierarchy of membership, with his fellow Illuminati occupying the upper tier. They targeted naïve but wealthy young men with their two-year program of self-confessionals, study, and secret fraternity. The novices moved up a level within that time, all the while using Illuminati contacts to advance their public careers. Weishaupt had created a kind of invisible college within existing schools, church offices, and institutions that held relatively progressive ideas. However, in-fighting developed among the various members of the upper tier, and thereafter had little influence.

Baron Adolf Franz Friederich Knigge joined the group in 1780. He belonged to the Freemasons and promoted the Illuminati in the older Order's underground network. He redesigned the Illuminati's inner workings to function on a more Masonic pattern, with additional graduations of membership and recruitment of many older, more powerful members from the Masonic ranks. Illuminati membership blossomed under Knigge and began to include nobility as well as influential thinkers and writers, such as the German philosopher Johann Wolfgang von Goethe.

“Members of the Order were investigated and made to endure show trials. Many were purged from public office after revealing details of the Illuminati's secret rituals and Satanic agenda.”

Anti-Illuminati sentiment

As the Illuminati became more popular, the authorities began to feel threatened. Bavaria's Duke Charles Theodore banned non-government fraternal and social groups in 1784, quite specifically naming the Order of the Illuminati as the reason for his action. Members of the Order were investigated and made to endure show trials. Many were purged from public office after revealing details of the Illuminati's secret rituals and Satanic agenda. One such member, Xavier Zwack, produced a large collection of papers detailing the godlessness of the Illuminati and its involvement in a multitude of crimes, including counterfeiting and abortion. All of this led to an official ban of the Illuminati in 1787.

"Robison codified the Illuminati as a secret plot to overthrow all religion and government in Europe and establish a New World Order."

The debate about its existence and practices continued though, and Illuminati-related literature sprang up, some of it written by surviving members such as Weishaupt, and much of the rest excerpted from the Zwack collection. Although the Order had been effectively crushed, its very nature as a secret group ensured its longevity in the public's mind, and forced it more deeply underground. For a while, the Illuminati took the blame for all manner of political scandal and public ill. This reached a crescendo

PARANOID PROFILE: Robert Anton Wilson

Robert Anton Wilson, the pre-eminent scholar, chronicler and satirist of the Illuminati' s escapades and historical impact, with his co-author Robert Shea, created the *Illuminatus!* trilogy, widely regarded as the classic work on conspiracy. *Illuminatus!* captured the chaos and energetic mystery that attracted a large audience to the parapolitical realm in the late 1970s. The three books, *The Eye of the Pyramid*, *The Golden Apple* and *Leviathan*, became so popular they were adapted into a rock epic performed at London' s National Theatre, under the patronage of Queen Elizabeth II. Wilson' s 1986 play, *Wilhelm Reich in Hell* was staged at the Edmund Burke Theatre in Dublin.

Wilson also earned a global reputation as a philosopher and social critic, much of it from Illuminati-related themes in such expository works as *Cosmic Trigger: The Final Secret of the Illuminati* (1979); *The Illuminati Papers* (1980); *Masks of the Illuminati* (1981); *Right Where You Are Sitting Now* (1983); *Quantum Psychology* (1990); *Nature' s God* (1991); *Everything Is Under Control: Conspiracies, Cults, and Cover-ups* (1998); *TSOG: The Thing That Ate the Constitution*(2002). His futurological ideas and sharp-witted insight into the state of the world have exerted an influence on cultural icons as diverse as Timothy Leary and George Carlin, and he remains one of the most articulate alternative voices in America.

The Illuminatus! trilogy chronicles an ever-widening conspiracy that starts with the disappearance of an editor of a leftist magazine that had published exposés on political assassinations of the 1960s. The plot involves a secret group called the Discordians, which alternately serves as an ally and an adversary to another secret group, the Illuminati. The goal of the Illuminati is to wreak havoc on society in order to "immanentize the Eschaton" and provide enlightenment and immortality for its members. To do this, the Illuminati attempt to start a nuclear war on an island called Fernando Poo, develop a strain of anthrax in order to create a plague, and attempt to revive the Nazi army. "Immanentizeing the Eschaton" borrows language from a Discordian religious cult that Wilson helped develop with friends Greg Hill and Kerry Thornley. Thornley had written a book about his experience serving in the Marines with Lee Harvey Oswald – published one year prior to the Kennedy assassination. The frenetic universe of Illuminatus!

in the bloody aftermath of the French Revolution of 1790, when a Mason named John Robison published *Proofs of Conspiracy*. Robison codified the Illuminati as a secret plot to overthrow all religion and government in Europe and establish a New World Order. Specifically, he maintained that two Illuminati-connected French politicians, Honore Mirabeau and Charles Maurice de Talleyrand-Perigord, had imposed the Order's secret plans in lodges throughout France, including the Jacobins who were responsible for the Reign of Terror following the French Revolution.

A Jesuit priest named Augustin Barruél constructed a more detailed history of the connections between the Jacobins and the Illuminati, entitled *Memoirs Illustrating the History of Jacobinism*, linking them to previous secret organizations, such as the Knights Templar and the Rosicrucians. Barruél declared that Francois-Marie Arouet Voltaire, Jean Jacques Rousseau, and Baron de Montesquieu had conspired against the church with false notions of liberty, equality, and fraternity. These first Illuminati conspiracy theorists tainted the revolutionary zeal of the Enlightenment in the eyes of many by planting the suspicion of an evil agenda. The murderous

coupled with the Discordian worship of Eris, a goddess of chaos, propelled both to underground cult status that has enthralled readers for decades. Offshoot cults included the Church of the Subgenius, with its pipe-smoking "Bob" (J. R. "Bob" Dobbs) icon, and which promote a parody of apocalyptic religious themes that enjoy enormous currency in a pop culture underground.

Wilson was born on January 18, 1932 in Brooklyn, New York. He worked as an associate editor for *Playboy* magazine from 1966-71, and some of what is found in Illuminatus! came from letters and information sent to him there. For many years, after the publication of Illuminatus! Wilson traveled widely lecturing on various philosophical issues connected to themes found in the book. He produced a staggering output of expository prose, primarily promoting an optimistic, futurist view of humanity, based in part on Timothy Leary' s models of the advancing intelligence of the human brain. Also a great enthusiast of the writer James Joyce, Wilson lived for a while in Ireland. He currently resides in southern California.

Wilson calls the Illuminati simply "a secret society in Bavaria in the eighteenth century". His conclusions about it, however, reflect on how a secret society with an ongoing impact on world events endures: "A certain number of paranoid individuals believe the Illuminati still exists and has either taken over the world, or taken over most of the world, or something like that. I discovered the anti-Illuminati literature in the late 60s when there were all sorts of weird conspiracy theories going around. And then I discovered there were two ambiguities connected with the Illuminati. First, there are those who say the Illuminati does not exist, versus those who say the Illuminati still exists. There are two schools of thought: those who claim they are the arch-villains of all history, and those who claim they are heroes trying to liberate the human race from superstition and ignorance. And so, I decided a group that is ambiguous, where we do not know whether they exist or not, and we do not know whether they are the good guys or the bad guys is the perfect symbol for all the confusions of the age we are living through, and all the rampant paranoia of our time. Conspiracy theories have never been more popular, not even in Nazi Germany."

Jacobins were considered to have not simply demonstrated fanatical excess but true Satanic underpinning of political progress. Barruél also argued that, like the modern day Al-Qaeda terrorists, the Bavarian Illuminati had planted sleeper cells in America to incite violent revolution.

Barruél's words, and those of John Robison when his *Proofs of Conspiracy* was reprinted in America, were well received among New England Federalists. One powerful cleric, Jedidiah Morse of First Church in Charlestown, Massachusetts, publicly declared Thomas Jefferson as the head of the Order of the Illuminati in America. Conveniently, Jefferson was also the chief rival to Federalist John Adams for the office of the presidency. Many other religious and political leaders, as well as newspaper editors and pundits, jumped on the anti-Illuminati bandwagon. Yet disapproval of the Order never led to an official ban in the United States.

> "These first Illuminati conspiracy theorists tainted the revolutionary zeal of the Enlightenment in the eyes of many by planting the suspicion of an evil agenda."

The idea of the Illuminati continued to capture the imagination. Barruél's book became popular in 1820s' France when the restored monarchy ruled, in contrast to the unstable times following the Revolution. (In contrast, anti-Illuminati crusades in the United States *circa* 1800 faded with the Federalist Party within a decade.)

Illuminati in the French Revolution

In 1919, Nesta Webster wrote, *The French Revolution – A Study In Democracy*, reviving the notion that the French Revolution had been accomplished more by the Bavarian Illuminati than the French. She claimed that in 1771 Adam Weishaupt had received instruction in ancient Egyptian occultism from a mysterious man named Kohlmer. Webster wrote extensively about secret societies, revolutions, and anti-Jewish, pro-fascist theories of history, although her support of Nazism ceased after the signing of the Hitler-Stalin pact. Webster died in 1960 and some consider her writings as having interested US political groups of the 1950s and 60s in the Illuminati. In 1996, the John Birch Society magazine *New American* ran articles arguing that French revolutionists had been recruited into the Illuminati through a convention of Freemasons attended by Mirabeau. Popular American television evangelist Pat Robertson wrote in his 1991 book *New World Order* that Illuminati members were recruited from the Rothschild banking family through a lodge in Frankfurt, Germany. Most famously, in 1975, the Illuminati inspired a three-

volume satire entitled *Illuminatus!* by authors Robert Shea and Robert Anton Wilson, the celebrated philosopher and futurist.

The Illuminati have since become the catch-all villains of many a conspiracy theory. Conspiracy theorists have identified them as every baddie from the corporate globalists to the minions of Satan himself. Aside from the historical group and its many imitators, the word "illuminati" with a small "i" often now describes inner circles any grander plot. The Grand Zionist conspiracy, for instance, has an "illuminati" consisting of the Rothschilds; an "illuminati" of Truman administration officials allegedly covered up the Roswell incident. A certain irony attends the fact that a name meant to suggest an enlightened elite has thus become widely regarded proverbially as a great conspiratorial force lurking in the shadows.

Above: Louis XVI was beheaded by the guillotine after the French Revolution.

LOS ANGELES

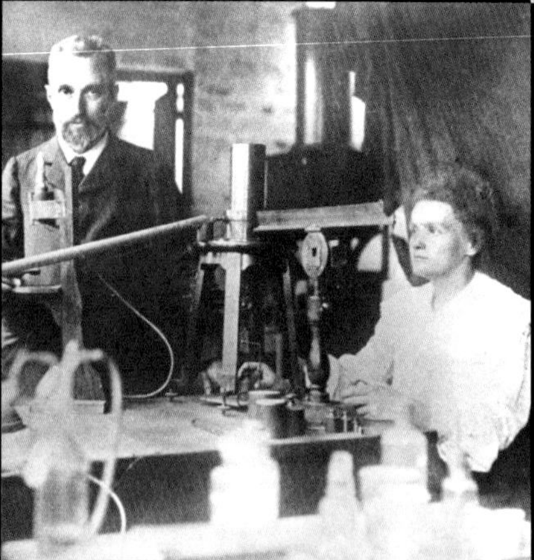

MEET
THE
PRESS

New World Order

The phrase "New World Order" adorns everything from old money to recent presidential speeches. To see the global culture of conspiracy that arose at the end of the last century and the beginning of this one, the reader need only review well-known and relatively recent events with an eye turned toward conspiracy.

Who shot JFK?

American President John F. Kennedy was assassinated on November 22, 1963, as his limousine drove past the Texas School Book Depository in Dealey Plaza, Dallas. Thousands looked on as the fatal shots were fired, yet still, decades later, no one can agree on what really happened that day.

Right: President John F. Kennedy.

The official story, according to the Warren Commission set up to investigate the incident, is that a lone gunman fired the shots from a building behind the president's motorcade. However, despite significant evidence supporting this explanation, countless skeptics have remained dissatisfied by this theory for almost half a century. Alternate theories about the assassination are so widespread that, in 2005, the satirical newspaper *The Onion* produced a parodic front page with the headline, "Kennedy Slain By CIA, Mafia, Castro, LBJ, Teamsters, Freemasons; President Shot 129 Times from 43 Different Angles."

Conflicting evidence

While there is generally no doubt that Lee Harvey Oswald was the man who fired the shots from the book depository, it is widely believed that he did not act under his own initiative. It is also suspected that he was not the only person to have fired shots at the president that day. Whatever did happen, there is now substantial evidence to suggest that attempts were made to cover up the real background to the events of November 22, 1963.

The most convincing piece of evidence in support of conspiracy theories is the home movie taken from the street by dressmaker Abraham Zapruder. While autopsy reports state that Kennedy was shot from behind, the film shows clearly that Kennedy was also shot from in front—by a shooter positioned behind the famed "grassy knoll." The bullet makes contact with the president's right temple, pushing him back and to the left. Despite the implications of the film, it was not used as evidence at the time, and was not shown on television until comedian-activist Dick Gregory and photographic expert Robert Groden brought it to the attention of TV reporter Geraldo Rivera in 1975.

This evidence was further obfuscated when *Life* magazine printed some of the Zapruder frames on its cover—reversed. This confusion persisted: In covering the event for CBS, reporter Dan Rather gave a verbal description that was more in keeping with the reversed scenes on the *Life* magazine cover than what was actually caught on film.

Did the Mafia want JFK dead?

So who was responsible for the shooting? Initial rumors implicated the Mafia—who resented Kennedy's tough stance on organized crime—but it seems inconceivable that even the most organized criminal group could have covered up their involvement for so long. They could, it is true, have provided the hitmen. The shooting of Lee Harvey Oswald on live television by petty mobster Jack Ruby is an obvious link to the Mob—but too obvious for many, who regard it as a "double bluff" that actually strengthens the case for the existence of a deeper conspiracy.

Below: Re-enactment of the assassination of JFK seen through a rifle telescope from the position occupied by Zapruder.

Lyndon B. Johnson's interest in the Vietnam War

Some researchers suspect that Lyndon Baines Johnson, the man who succeeded Kennedy as president, had some role to play in JFK's murder. Proponents of this theory include Barr McClellan, author of *Blood, Money and Power: How LBJ killed JFK*; Craig Zirbel, in *The Texas Connection*; and Johnson's mistress Madeleine Duncan Brown, in *Texas in the Morning: The Love Story of Madeleine Brown and President Lyndon Johnson*. This theory presents Johnson's accession to the White House as an obvious motive for the assassination, but also draws on Kennedy's increasing frustration with the Vietnam War, which had seen him begin to withdraw advisers from Vietnam and to consider abandoning the war effort altogether.

"one of Johnson's first acts as president was to sign a national security action memorandum that reversed JFK's policies."

Many scenarios suggest Johnson might have been motivated not only by ambition, but also as an agent of the Military-Industrial Complex, an amalgam of Pentagon contractors and big oil corporations with a vested interest in prolonging the Vietnam War. In fact, one of Johnson's first acts as president was to sign a national security action memorandum (NSAM number 273) that reversed JFK's decision to begin withdrawing troops from the warzone

CONSPIRACY LINKS:

Fidel Castro

Following America's failed invasion of Cuba at the Bay of Pigs on April 15, 1961, President John F. Kennedy set plans in motion to overthrow Fidel Castro by covert means. The project was named "Operation Mongoose," and was put under the charge of Brigadier General Edward Lansdale. Along with Brigadier General William Craig, Lansdale initiated a series of projects intended to discredit Castro, which are alleged to have included faking evidence to suggest Castro's forces had sabotaged Florida space launches, and of a planned attack on the U.S. militay base at Guantanamo Bay.

Plot and Counterplot

Some of Lansdale's projects may have originated in conversations he had with JFK, and some researchers conclude that the president may have given his approval to plans to kill Castro.

The Cuban dictator made a clear effort to connect these plots with official U.S. government policy. There is some evidence that he was successful: On the very day that a potential Castro assassin, Rolando Cubela, was to have a meeting at CIA headquarters, Castro made a public statement from the Brazilian embassy, where Cubela had met with a U.S. contact on a previous occasion. This choice of location and timing might suggest that Castro knew more than he was admitting about the plots against him, and about their origins in the White House.

Further evidence of Castro's growing enmity with JFK came in an interview with Associate Press reporter Daniel Harker on September 7, 1963, when he said, "United States leaders should think that if they are aiding terrorist plans to eliminate Cuban leaders, they themselves will not be safe."

(NSAM number 263). Military hardware manufacturers and big oil companies profited enormously from the continuation of the war. Over the years, many of Johnson's inner circle, including his self-confessed long-term mistress Madeleine Brown, have attested to his attendance at secret meetings with powerful oil executives just prior to JFK's murder.

Was Johnson one of "The Guilty Men"?

Speculation that JFK's successor was somehow involved in his assassination has been fueled over the years by continuing attempts to censor independent investigation. Consider, for instance, the recent withdrawal of a JFK assassination documentary broadcast on the History Channel in the United States. The documentary, called "The Guilty Men," was just one instalment of a series called "The Men Who Killed Kennedy," which examined various theories regarding the assassination. Other episodes aired with little controversy until "The Guilty Men," which focused on the theory that Lyndon B. Johnson was responsible for the assassination, drawing inspiration from Bar McClellan's recent book, *Blood, Money & Power*.

According to the book, the assassination was arranged by Ed Clark, who became Johnson's ambassador to Australia in 1965. As evidence supporting Johnson's involvement, McClellan cites a fingerprint taken at the book depository that, through modern forensic science, can now be matched to a man called Mac Wallace. In 1952 Wallace was given a suspended five-year sentence for the murder of John Kinser, the boyfriend of Johnson's sister Josefa. And

CIA apologists have long held that this threat suggests Castro was involved in JFK's assassination. It seems more likely, however, that Castro was simply alerting Washington to his knowledge of Operation Mongoose. It is now thought that Cubela, Castro's supposed potential assassin, may in fact have been a double agent on assignment from Havana to find out where the responsibility for the plots ended.

According to some, a back-channel diplomatic rapprochement had been taking place between Kennedy and Castro. If this is true, it suggests that Castro came to belive that responsibility for Operation Mongoose did not reach all the way to the top, but rested with a Pentagon intelligence cell that included Lansdale and Craig. In that case, involvement of the Cuban leader in the death of JFK must be considered extremely unlikely.

Above: Fidel Castro, photographed in 1959.

Above: Lee Harvey Oswald, the man accused of murdering JFK, is shot dead by Jack Ruby in a Dallas Police Station.

in 1963, Wallace was implicated in the murder of Henry Marshall, chief investigator in a corruption scandal that had threatened to ruin Johnson's career. For McClellan, this was sufficient evidence to suggest that Wallace was Johnson's hired gun, and that he had shot and killed JFK

McClellan was by no means the first to consider Johnson's involvement, and not even the first to discuss the possibility on "The Men Who Killed Kennedy" series. However, this particular program seemed to strike a nerve. After a single broadcast of "The Guilty Men," the History Channel announced that the program would not receive another airing, and would not be available on DVD. It is believed that the cable channel was influenced by a co-ordinated letter-writing campaign mounted by three powerful men: Bill Moyers, a public television commentator who at one time served as Johnson's press secretary; Jack Valenti, a former head of the Motion Picture Association of America and one-time adviser to Johnson; and former president Gerald R. Ford, who served on the Warren Commission enquiry into the death of JFK and, according to some researchers, worked with the FBI. What could have prompted such a response from men like this?

Why focus on McClellan?

Was McClellan too close to the truth with his theory? Film director Oliver Stone had made similar claims in his movie *JFK* without

POINTS TO PONDER: LEE HARVEY OSWALD

- Many conspiracy theories about the assassination of JFK are kept alive by the curious number of coincidences relating to Lee Harvey Oswald.
- Oswald pursued a highly visible public life as an exaggerated, almost stereotypical Marxist, handing out "Fair Play for Cuba" pamphlets in support of Fidel Castro, getting into brawls in the street and vigorous debates on the radio.
- Some people consider that he "protested too much," and that these exaggerated displays of political dissent were a front to cover up his real affiliations and implicate Castro in the assassination.
- Oswald served in the Marines at the Atsugi Air Force base, from where the U2 spy plane flew its missions. He worked in a high-security area tracking the plane's flight patterns.
- In October 1959, he defected to the former Soviet Union. The embassy official that processed his request was also responsible for monitoring Soviet reaction to U2 flights.
- Oswald appealed to the same embassy official in February 1961, and asked for and received the return of his U.S. citizenship.
- After returning to the United States, but before getting his job at the Dallas Book Depository, Oswald worked at Jaggar-Chiles-Stovall, a photographic lab that processed U2 surveillance film.
- Multiple Oswalds appeared all over Dallas in the period just before November 22, 1963. An Oswald look-alike defected to the Soviet Union at the same time as the known one. A man calling himself Oswald appeared and was photographed and recorded at the U.S. embassy in Mexico.
- Cutting-edge JFK researchers suggest that an Oswald double may have been around since his childhood, and that both may have been recruited to take part in the assassination. It all suggests a far more sophisticated operation than the lone gunman theory that the Warren Commission intended the world to believe.

attracting censorship. Dozens, if not hundreds, of similar swipes at Johnson had come out of the "cottage industry" that the Kennedy-assassination media had become in the decades since the event. So why were Moyers, Valenti, and Ford moved to challenge the History Channel on this occasion?

One theory is that it had something to do with Barr McClellan's son, Scott. Scott McClellan replaced Ari Fleischer as the White House press secretary in July 2003, leading some commentators to suspect that the elder McClellan's book contained inside information not available to other writers on the subject. To these theorists, the suppression of "The Guilty Men" was another demonstration of how government bureaucracy could work across supposedly oppositional party lines to cover up past scandal.

Modern presidents

Since the Vietnam War and the death of JFK, conspiracy theories have sprung up around almost every U.S. president. How many of them are based in fact, and how many are mere speculation? And what is behind this erosion of trust between a people and their government?

Right: The north facade of the White House.

In 1865, eight people were convicted of conspiring to murder Abraham Lincoln. But by 1963, any challenge to the accepted story of the death of JFK met significant official resistance. Conspiracy theories regarding the governing regime in the U.S. had become taboo, giving birth to a general cynicism that was reinforced in the year 2000 by a presidential race decided in the courthouse rather than at the ballot box. The conspiracy theories surrounding modern presidents are symptomatic of this public disenchantment.

The attempted assassination of President Reagan

President George H. W. Bush Senior is the former head of the CIA, and was vice president for two terms under Ronald Reagan. According to the Associated Press (March 31, 1981), one of Bush's sons, Neil, was scheduled to lunch with the brother of Reagan's would-be assassin on the very day of the assassination attempt. This co-incidence has generated theories that perhaps Bush Senior was tempted to accelerate his succession to the Oval Office using the tried-and-true CIA technique of assassination.

The First Gulf War

Bush Senior's presidency was marked by an ambiguous attitude to the military power of Saddam Hussein. The U.S. Ambassador to Iraq, April Glaspie, told Saddam in 1990 that "We have no opinion on your Arab-Arab conflicts, such as your dispute with Kuwait . . . the Kuwait issue is not associated with America." This was taken by the Iraqi leader as a green light to invade Kuwait, and as a result might be regarded to have precipitated the first Gulf War.

Iran-Contra Affair

In Reagan's famous "mistakes were made" speech, he admitted that in 1986, members of his administration (including Oliver North, John Poindexter, Otto Reich, Dick Cheney, and Robert Gates) negotiated the sale of arms to Iran—an enemy of the United States—in exchange for the release of hostages. However, for many, justice was never seen to be done. Reagan denied that the profits of these sales had been diverted to fund the Contras, an anti-communist guerrilla organization in Nicaragua, and the Iran-Contra (or Iran-gate) scandal wound down under the administration of George W. Bush with few prosecutions.

One of those prosecuted was John Poindexter (whose convictions were overturned in court in 1991), who went on to serve in George W. Bush's administration in an office known as Total Information Awareness. He was forced to resign in August 2003 after a public scandal erupted over a system he had developed to profiteer from terrorist activity, using the futures market to bet on developments in the Middle East. Poindexter was just one of several Iran-Contra players to serve under George W. Bush.

President Bill Clinton could also be regarded as an Iran-Contra alumnus, according to conspiracy theorists such as Terry Reed. In his book *Compromised*, Reed alleges that, long before his celebrated sex scandals, Clinton was known to have been involved in the cover-up of a guns-and-drugs trafficking route between Nicaragua and the

Below:
Chaos surrounds the victims after the assassination attempt on President Reagan, March 30, 1981.

little town of Mena, Arkansas. The operation was one of many run by the most notorious Iran-Contra convict of them all, Oliver North. Reed goes on to suggest that, by intervening to prevent any serious investigation of the Mena airstrip affair, Clinton may have endeared himself to the Reagan/Bush team, and helped establish himself to them as an acceptable alternative as president if Bush Senior were to lose the forthcoming election.

Sleeping with the enemy: The "October Surprise"

The Iran-Contra scandal continued a theme of "sleeping-with-the-enemy" played out between Iran and the new era of American conservatism ushered in by Reagan. This theme began with the infamous "October Surprise," whereby the Ayatollah Khomeini was allegedly paid to delay the release of 52 American hostages held by Iran until after the 1980 presidential vote. The hostages were eventually released on the very day that Reagan was sworn in as president. According to reporters such as Harry Martin of the *NAPA Valley Sentinel*, the pay-off to the Ayatollah amounted to US$40 million.

"the pay-off to the Ayatollah amounted to US$40 million."

Delivery of this money was tied up with the illegal sale of the super-surveillance software, known as PROMIS, to police agencies worldwide. Investigation of the payments culminated in the Inslaw scandal, regarded by many conspiracy theorists as the Rosetta stone of modern presidential parapolitics. The scandal was uncovered by

CONSPIRACY LINKS:

Judah Philip Benjamin

Judah Philip Benjamin (1811–1884) was the highest-placed Jewish politician in the history of the United States. He served as Senator for Louisiana from 1853 until 1861, when Louisiana seceeded and joined the southern Confederacy. Benjamin then served as Attorney General to the Confederacy under its President, Jefferson Davis, and went on to become its Secretary of War and Secretary of State.

Benjamin fled to Great Britain after the capture of Jefferson Davis in 1865, and he enjoyed a successful legal career in exile. The Crown appointed him Queen's Counsel for Lancashire in 1872 after he wrote an influential treatise on personal property law. He retired in 1883.

Many historians agree, however, that Judah P. Benjamin bled the American South dry of its financial assets during the Civil War, transferring substantial sums to British banks. Some even argue that this was a decisive factor in the South's defeat. Judah Phillip Benjamin was the only member of the Confederate government never to return to the United States. He died in Paris in 1884.

Other theorists suspect Benjamin of being complicit in the murder of Abraham Lincoln. The story goes that Lincoln's assassin, John Wilkes Booth, worked as an agent for the Confederate secret service, as part of a group that intended to kidnap Lincoln and blow up the White House. Wilkes's covert team worked at the behest of the defeated Confederate leaders, including Benjamin. Their plans, which Benjamin may have helped to formulate, had nothing to do with an attempt to return to power, but were rather attempts at revenge for the defeated South.

writer Danny Casolaro just before his own mysterious death in 1992. (See pages 72–82 for more details on these events.)

A paragon of Fair Play?

President Jimmy Carter won office over Gerald Ford in 1977, when Ford's secret deal to pardon Richard Nixon's crimes came to light, wrecking his chances of re-election. Even the most avid conspiracy theorists struggle to find evidence of any shady dealings in Carter's election, and his time in office has attracted very little controversy.

Carter did, however, back-pedal on one compaign issue after his election—that of UFOs. He told reporters of his own UFO sighting during his election campaign of 1976: "It was the darnedest thing I've ever seen. It was big, it was very bright, it changed colors and it was about the size of the moon. We watched it for ten minutes, but none of us could figure out what it was. One thing is for sure, I'll never make fun of people who say they've seen unidentified objects in the sky. If I become President, I'll make every piece of information this country has about UFO sightings available to the public and the scientists." (as reported in Timothy Good's book, *Above Top Secret*). Official revelations regarding UFOs were, however, notably absent from his time in office.

The only other conspiracy cloud on the horizon of Carter's time in office was brought to public notice by his security advisor, Zbigniew Brzezinski. Brzezinski asserts that in July 1979, Carter signed the first American directive to supply aid to opponents of the Soviet regime in Afghanistan. Those opponents were known as the *mujahaddin*, an organization that was later to evolve into Al-Qaeda.

Above: Judah Philip Benjamin, circa 1860.

Regardless of the truth of these accusations, they have had a lasting effect on the attitude of many Americans toward Jewish politicians. In the U.S. presidential campaign of 2000, incumbent Vice President Al Gore selected Connecticut Senator Joseph Lieberman as his running partner. Lieberman was Jewish, and with the planned declaration of a Palestinian state in September of that year, the idea of a Jewish man second-in-command to the American presidency was certain to attract controversy.

Within a week of Lieberman's selection, the Dallas branch of the National Association for the Advancement of Colored People (NAACP), a black civil rights group, forced its president to resign after he called Lieberman "very suspicious" and complained of Jews that "their interest primarily has to do with money and these kinds of things."

Above: Participator in a rally, held in New York, on February 23, 1970. The rally was organized to protest the violent police response to political demonstrations held at the Chicago Democratic Convention

POINTS TO PONDER: WALLACE AND ASHCROFT

- One of Nixon's most prominent rivals, presidential candidate George Wallace, was put out of the race and left paralyzed by an attempted assassination in 1972. The attempt has since been linked to certain members of Nixon's campaign team.
- Timothy W. Maier and James P. Lucier theorize, in their book "Insight on the News," that President Richard Nixon may have ordered the Secret Service not to investigate the 1972 Wallace shooting, although declassified records obtained by "news alert!" have since shown agents went against Nixon's orders and continued to look for a conspiracy without success.
- John Ashcroft, the 79th Attorney General of the United States, was frequently criticized for uneven prosecutions under oppressive legislation known as the Patriot Acts I and II.
- Ashcroft's earliest failures in the Bush Administration were the post-9/11 anthrax letters. In December 2001, following the 9/11 attacks, moderately progressive office holders, such as Democratic Senators Tom Daschle and Patrick Leahy, received letters tainted with deadly anthrax bacteria in a series of incidents that triggered widespread panic. Ashcroft's office never found or prosecuted anyone over these incidents.

Watergate

Richard Nixon resigned from office rather than face an inquiry into allegations against him, the most notable among them relating to the 1972 break-in at the National Headquarters of the Democratic Party at the Watergate Hotel in Washington DC.

However, historians agree that the burglary at the Watergate was an amateurish crime and totally unnecessary to Nixon's pursuit of power. This has led to the argument that Nixon was set up for his fall at Watergate, evidenced by the fact that the door at the hotel had been duct-taped open in so obvious a manner that it essentially invited the police to discover the burglaries.

Presidential election unrest

Nixon came to power in 1968 with a landside defeat of Democratic candidate Hubert Humphrey. Before his spell as L.B. Johnson's Vice President, Humphrey was known in the political realm as leader of the liberal wing of the Democratic Party. Riots broke out at the Democratic National Convention in Chicago that year because Humphrey's Democrats espoused a policy on the Vietnam War that was even less popular than that of the Republicans.

The violence began after the "Yippies" (or "young" "hippies"), led by Abbie Hoffman and Jerry Rubin, arranged a protest against Humphrey's Vietnam policies. The protest passed peacefully until Chicago Mayor Richard Daley—a prominent supporter of Humphrey—called on the police to attack peaceful protesters. This was neither the first nor the last "police riot" to occur in the 1960s.

Humphrey became the Democratic candidate by default, after the assassination of Robert F. Kennedy during the primary election season, leading some to posit his involvement in the deaths of one or both Kennedy brothers. However, no evidence to this effect has yet been produced, and the theory remains on the lunatic fringe.

George W. Bush and 9/11

With George W. Bush in the White House, the fervor surrounding theories of presidential conspiracy reached new heights. George W. Bush was the first American president appointed by judicial appointment rather than free election. Liberals and Conservatives alike noted that an aberration in the traditional American route to power had emerged. By the end of his first term, Bush had brought the USA to war, and created confusion among the public regarding Iraq's connection to Al-Qaeda, and its possession or not of weapons of mass destruction. Public discontent with government policy, and charges of corruption surrounding many public offices, added to general mistrust.

PEOPLE IN PURSUIT:

Michael Moore

Michael Moore's 2004 documentary *Fahrenheit 911* made its impact on the global conspiracy cognoscenti by offering information about a man named James Bath. In the film, Moore presented documentation that George W. Bush and Bath had served together in the military forces. Conspiracy theorists had long known Bath was a money conduit between the Bush family and oil-millionaires in Saudi Arabia, a connection most notably spelled out in a book by Peter Brewton entitled *The Mafia, CIA and George Bush*.

Bath was, in fact, closely associated with Adnan Khashoggi, who was not only an arms merchant linked to the Iran-Contra scandal, but was also uncle to Dodi Al Fayed and suspected of being involved in the deaths of Dodi and Princess Diana. Khashoggi brokered a series of contracts between the Saudi government and the British aerospace industry.

Immediately after the 9/11 attacks, members of the Bin Laden family were flown out of the United States, at a time when all other air traffic was stopped. Michael Moore was criticized by writer Christopher Hitchens for failing to mention Richard Clarke in the film, the person who claimed responsibility for approving those flights. Clarke became a critic of the Bush administration, particularly over its failure with regard to terrorist threats prior to 9/11. Hitchens's criticism of Moore's off-screen defense of Clarke begged an

Left: Richard Nixon leaving the White House after his resignation from office following the Watergate affair.

important question: what difference does it make which functionary of the Administration approved such an action?

Other areas investigated by Moore include the mysterious deaths of a number of key Democratic politicians. *Fahrenheit 911* refers to the death of Mel Carnahan, the Governor of Missouri, in an unusual plane crash during the 2000 elections. Carnahan had been running against John Ashcroft, who in fact failed to win even after Carnahan's death. Bush subsequently appointed Ashcroft Attorney General. The movie does not mention, however, another plane crash that killed Minnesota Senator Paul Wellstone during the next congressional election year and resulted in a crucial political loss to Bush's opponents. Coincidence lurks further in the past: in 1976 a plane crash killed another midwestern politician, Missouri's Jerry Litton, abruptly ending his bid for a seat in the Senate. The seat went instead to long-time Bush ally John Danforth. Danforth had served as a mentor to Justice Clarence Thomas, a key member of the Supreme Court that appointed George H. W. Bush. Danforth went on to become Bush's appointee as U.S. Ambassador to the United Nations.

RFK must die!

Robert F. Kennedy was shot and killed as he announced his victory in the 1968 California presidential primary. In a grim echo of his brother's assassination, a lone, obsessive gunman was found guilty of his murder. But were madness and obsession the real motives for the killing, or were more sinister forces at work?

Right: RFK addressing a crowd at the Ambassador Hotel just before the shooting.

Robert F. Kennedy was shot and fatally wounded during a visit to the Ambassador Hotel in Los Angeles on June 5, 1968. In his autopsy report, coroner Thomas Noguchi determined that the bullets had been fired into RFK's skull from close enough to leave powder burns behind his ear. A few miles away, police held Sirhan Sirhan, the man suspected of the shooting, in custody.

While Sirhan had certainly fired a number of shots at Kennedy, eyewitnesses claimed that he had been standing much further away than the autopsy report suggested—at least five feet (1.5 meters) in front of the victim—when the shots were fired. Despite eyewitness accounts and forensic evidence suggesting his innocence, Sirhan remained the only suspect in the case, and was ultimately found guilty. But did Sirhan actually kill RFK? And if so, could he have acted alone?

Why kill Robert F. Kennedy?

Robert Kennedy had made many enemies in the course of his political career. In the 1950s his leadership of a congressional committee investigation of labor unions led to a well-publicized clash with labor leader Jimmy Hoffa. Prior to that, he had served on the staff of Senator Joseph McCarthy during his infamous Communist witch-hunts. As a politician, RFK had managed his brother's presidential campaign in 1960, and was Attorney General in JFK's administration. He left the post after his brother's assassination in 1963, winning senatorial office in New York.

However, RFK's major threat to the establishment at the time of

Left: Sirhan Sirhan, charged with the assassination of RFK

his assassination had to do with the Vietnam War. He was the peace candidate, publicly discussing pulling America out of Vietnam and therefore reversing a military build-up initiated by Lyndon Johnson after JFK's death.

According to William Turner and John Christian in *The Assassination of Robert F. Kennedy*, RFK also secretly planned to prosecute people within the government for his brother's murder. This may have provided another motive to silence him.

POINTS TO PONDER: DID SIRHAN ACT ALONE?

- There is no doubt that Sirhan Sirhan could have been a potential enemy—he was a Palestinian immigrant from Jerusalem, ostensibly with an extremist opposition to the senator's policies regarding Israel—but was he responsible for killing Kennedy?
- Although Sirhan shot eight bullets, a total of 12 were recovered from the scene, and a "magic bullet" theory has not yet been offered to explain this.
- Sirhan was wrestled to the ground in front of the senator, yet Kennedy was shot from behind.
- A woman in a polka-dot dress was seen talking with Sirhan before the murder and leaving the scene afterward declaring "We shot Kennedy!" She was never found or questioned.
- The gun belonging to a security guard standing beside Kennedy at the time of the shooting was drawn at the time but was never entered as evidence in the case.

Right: The .22 revolver with which RFK was fatally shot by Sirhan.

Was Sirhan hypnotized?

One of the key exhibits in Sirhan's trial was a page from his journal, on which phrases such as "RFK must die! RFK must die! RFK must die!" had been written repeatedly. The unhinged nature of the writing reflects the possibility that Sirhan was a victim of mind control. Sirhan writes elsewhere in his journal that his need to kill Kennedy was "an unshakable obsession." In interviews during the investigation, it became clear to psychiatrists that Sirhan had been hypnotized in the past, probably many times, and was an ideal candidate for mind control. Dr. L. Diamond, the chief psychiatrist for the defense, used hypnosis on Sirhan, and the subject proved so susceptible that Diamond concluded Sirhan had likely been hypnotized a number of times previously. Under hypnosis, Sirhan displayed the same manner of writing that appeared in his journal.

Witnesses additionally claim that Sirhan acted as though in a hypnotic state during the shooting. He claims to have been led to the room where Kennedy was shot, after which he said he blacked out—he himself had no recollection of the shooting. The case for mind control is so strong that Sirhan's lawyer, Lawrence Teeters, approached his parole board with it and has requested it be admitted as evidence for the defense in any new trial. However, Sirhan is currently serving a life sentence in California, and as of 2007 has been denied parole 13 times.

Muted official response

It is perhaps less a cause for suspicion than for sadness that Bobby Kennedy's murder—unlike that of his brother—has received little official recognition. What has prevented the site of Kennedy's shooting from becoming a permanent memorial to a great leader and this tragically momentous event? The Lorraine Hotel in Memphis, Tennessee, where Martin Luther King Jr. was shot, now houses a civil rights museum. In Dallas, the infamous "grassy knoll" now serves as a shrine to JFK, and the Texas School Book Depository stands as a museum. Yet, at the Ambassador Hotel on Wilshire Boulevard in Los Angeles, weeds climb the walls of a boarded-up building. Barbed wire and a chain-link fence keep prying eyes away.

In November 2004, the current owners of the hotel, the Los Angeles Board of Education, voted to demolish most of the historic locale and convert the rest into a small campus. The only concession to the history that was made and broken there has been the formation of a five-member panel to decide how the pantry where Kennedy was shot will be used.

Death of Princess Diana

News of the death of Diana, Princess of Wales, was greeted with shock and grief around the world. While it seems inconceivable that Diana's death could have been anything but a tragic accident, many questions about the exact events surrounding it remain unanswered.

Right: Diana, Princess of Wales.

Intoxicated to some degree with alcohol, the sedative Tiapridal, and the antidepressant Prozac (according to blood samples reported by the BBC as well as medically-conclusive tests using fluid taken from the sclera as reported by the French authorities) chauffeur Henri Paul drove Diana, Princess of Wales and her paramour Dodi Al Fayed into the Pont D'Alma tunnel beneath the streets of Paris on August 31, 1997.

> "A string of unlikely coincidences and unanswered questions has led many theorists to suspect that the crash in the Pont D Alma tunnel was an orchestrated assassination."

Only the bodyguard, Trevor Rees-Jones, emerged from the tunnel without fatal injuries. The Mercedes sedan passed a white Fiat and, after a blinding flash, crashed violently into a concrete pillar at somewhere between 90 and 110 miles per hour (145 and 177 kilometers per hour). The car ricocheted off the pillar and smashed into the opposite wall. Paul and the 42-year-old Dodi Al Fayed died instantly. Paramedics gave 34-year-old Diana a blood transfusion at the scene, but her heart stopped in the ambulance en route to the hospital, where she died four hours later.

Despite a continuing public inquiry, Diana's death has provoked questions of conspiracy that endure to the present day. In the same way that authorities had declared JFK's murder the result of a single gunman acting alone, official investigations into Diana's death concluded that it was a simple car accident. And, as with JFK., a string of unlikely coincidences and unanswered questions has led many people to suspect that the crash in the Pont D'Alma tunnel was an orchestrated assassination, possibly carried out by MI6, the United Kingdom's external intelligence agency, on behalf of the British monarchy.

Religious conversion: motive for murder?

At the time of the accident, Diana was pursuing a relationship with an Egyptian, Dodi Al Fayed, a Muslim and the son of powerful businessman, Mohamed Al Fayed, who was himself at odds with the authorities in the United Kingdom. It has been suggested that Diana was pregnant with Dodi Al Fayed's child at the time of her death, and that the two may have been intending to marry following Diana's conversion to Islam. It is widely believed by conspiracy theorists that the prospect of Prince William, future king of England, having a Muslim mother and stepfather would be totally unacceptable to the Crown.

Why Pitie-Salpetriere Hospital?

Another unanswered question is why the ambulance took Diana to the Pitie-Salpetriere hospital, an hour and forty minutes drive away,

Below: Wreckage of the Mercedes S280 being removed from the Alma Underpass where Princess Diana and Dodi Al Fayed died.

Above: The underpass at the Pont D'Alma, Paris, France, in September 1997, soon after the death of Princess Diana and Dodi Al Fayed.

despite the closer proximity of four other hospitals. According to the U.S. government, the Pitie Salpetriere is the hospital of choice for officials visiting Paris. Yet conspiracy critics believe it houses a number of intelligence community operatives. French officials attribute the choice to the medics' inclination to try and stabilize the victim before proceeding to hospital, and as an attempt by the ambulance not to aggravate Diana's injuries.

How many more deaths?

Most disturbing is the evidence that a number of people closely investigating the case have also subsequently met with untimely deaths. The papparazzi photographer, James Andanson, who may have owned the white Fiat encountered in the tunnel, died in questionable circumstances in May 2000. Police discovered Andanson's burned body in a charred BMW in woodland near the village of Nant, in Aveyron in southwestern France. Previously, Andanson's Paris office had been burgled by three masked and well-trained men who wounded a security guard and, for a while, kept the office staff hostage. It took four weeks for police to identify Andanson's remains from DNA tests. Official investigators consider Andanson's death a suicide, despite the bizarre circumstances.

After Diana's death, American writer Jim Keith was among the first to suggest that she had been pregnant when she died, in his on-line column *Nitro News*. Keith promised to name the physician from whom the information came—reportedly Dodi al Fayed's own—but died suddenly before finishing his final column.

So suspicion surrounding the death of Diana endures. Dodi Al Fayed's father, Mohamed, has devoted tremendous resources to finding answers to these questions. Under pressure from Al Fayed, some official conclusions—including the alcohol toxicity levels in Henri Paul's blood—have been reconsidered. However, neither the 2004 investigation, nor the 2007 inquest into the deaths has yet reached a conclusion, and few people expect the whole truth ever to be revealed.

POINTS TO PONDER: UNANSWERED QUESTIONS

- What was the full extent of Diana's injuries? Early news reports had her up and walking around immediately after the crash, and reportedly the princess could still speak when paramedics arrived on the scene.
- Had the vehicle been tampered with? A few weeks prior to the accident, the Mercedes had been stolen from the garage of the Ritz hotel, where the fatal ride began. Police had recovered the car but found that some of its instrumentation had been adjusted. The car was reinspected and reconditioned shortly after.
- What was Trevor-Rees Jones's role in the affair? Contrary to normal bodyguard procedure, Trevor Rees-Jones fastened his seatbelt before the ride. The others did not. Rees-Jones later claimed amnesia about the event, due not to the trauma but to the drugs he received in the hospital for his severe facial injuries.
- Was Henri Paul an alcoholic? He appears sober in video footage taken at the Ritz hotel just before they entered the car. Friends and family challenge the notion that Paul had a severe alcohol problem, and no evidence of his supposed alcohol abuse was found in his flat.
- Was Henri Paul paid off? A mysterious US$200,000 had been deposited in Henri Paul's bank account just prior to the crash. A former MI6 agent named Richard Tomlinson claimed the money came from MI6.
- What exactly happened inside that tunnel? Seventeen cameras inside the tunnel failed to operate at the time of the crash.
- What role did the French authorities play? The French opened up the tunnel roadway only hours after the crash and neglected to collect important evidence. Many regard the apparent incompetence of otherwise experienced officers in the French investigation as a cause for continued speculation about conspiracy.

Left: Diana's coffin carried through London, England, on the day of her funeral, September 6, 1997.

Tentacles of global conspiracy

What if all conspiracies were connected by a single, immensely powerful secret order attempting to establish global government? Writer Danny Casolaro devoted his life to uncovering this secret, and some theorists believe he was murdered for getting too close to the truth.

Right: Spies and conspiracies abound in Casolaro's theory of global conspiracy.

By the time of his death in August 1992, writer Danny Casolaro had attempted to expose a number of rumored conspiracies, which he believed were connected by single group of powerful and ambitious men whom he refered to as the "Octopus."

These conspiracies included: the October Surprise of 1980 (see page 58); the Iran-Contra scandal (see page 56); ECHELON, the U.S. government's satellite spying system; the Nugan Hand international money laundering scandal in Australia; and above all the Inslaw scandal, which involved the theft and illegal sale of PROMIS, a high-tech tracking computer program sold illegally to police and intelligence agencies around the world.

Casolaro believed he had tapped into a global structure of conspiratorial manipulation, a many-tentacled creature he called "Octopus" that dealt in pan-global information gathering. But had Casolaro uncovered a device enabling global espionage? And if so, how—and why—did it become global?

PROMIS History

PROMIS stands for Prosecutors' Management Information Software, and was originally designed for use in tracking criminal cases through various jurisdictions. An American software development company named Inslaw originally developed it using a law enforcement assistance grant, and the St. Louis, Missouri Police Department conducted trials with an early version of it in the 1970s. The federal government was also interested in its potential: during the Vietnam War, a prototype of PROMIS was used to keep track of key members of the Viet Cong, who were then marked for assassination as part of a secret military operation named Phoenix.

In civilian use, PROMIS was intended to keep detailed profiles of known criminals and their movements, to allow prosecutors' offices to keep track of them. To this end, Inslaw sold its software to various police agencies in the U.S., but was not granted permission to modify or distribute the software outside federal government.

Long before Casolaro stumbled upon PROMIS as part of his research, the public assistance money had run out. However, Inslaw had continued to develop PROMIS, and eventually created a program containing over one million lines of code, making it an extremely flexible application.

One of these later developments involved prediction. When fed enormous amounts of data, PROMIS could predict a criminal's next move with uncanny accuracy. This version of PROMIS helped Navy submarines to navigate through previously unmappable icy regions of the Arctic sea. Spy satellites eventually would come to use a PROMIS function called "fractal framing" that extrapolated visual information in the pixels of long-distance imaging, allowing for the global surveillance now commonly available on Google Earth.

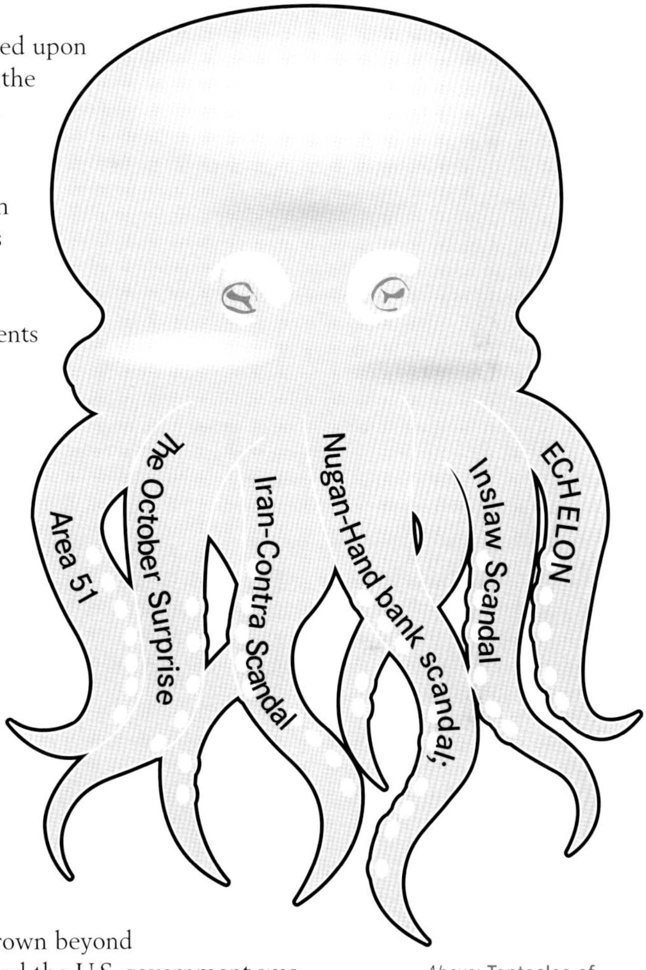

PROMIS's capabilities had grown beyond belief by the 1980s and 1990s, and the U.S. government was increasingly anxious to wrest control of its application from the company that developed it. It was the breaking of copyright restrictions on modifying and distributing this powerful piece of software that led to the Inslaw scandal, and the beginning of Casolaro's research. This was also the mechanism by which this ultimate information-gathering tool allegedly fell into the hands of America's most infamous enemy, Osama Bin Laden.

Above: Tentacles of global conspiracy. Danny Casolaro postulated the "Octopus" theory–all conspiracies linked together in one large global conspiracy.

The ability to predict is leaked

According to news stories that surfaced long after Casolaro died, the elusive Osama Bin Laden put PROMIS's prediction capabilities to effective use in his campaign against the United States. Bin Laden is alleged to have paid US$2 million for the software on the Russian black market, after it was sold to Russia by an FBI turncoat named Robert Hanssen.

> "Had he been using PROMIS, presumably against another PROMIS tracking system, Bin Laden could have extrapolated what his pursuers planned and would have moved on before the assault on Tora Bora."

PROMIS gave Bin Laden the ability to keep one step ahead of his pursuers. For example, he twice narrowly escaped missile strikes on his training camps, once in retaliation for the U.S. Embassy bombings in Nairobi in 1998, and again at the time of the bombing of USS *Cole* in 2000. In 2001, Bin Laden—labeled the world's most wanted terrorist—escaped capture at Tora Bora, a cave complex in eastern Afghanistan, despite advance intercepts that had given away his precise location. Use of a PROMIS system would have enabled him to predict the attacks and escape all attempts on his life.

PEOPLE IN PURSUIT:

Danny Casolaro

Joseph Daniel Casolaro was born in West Virginia in 1947. A passionate investigative reporter, he became fascinated by the Inslaw scandal–the legal wrangling between the U.S. Department of Justice, who owned PROMIS, and Inslaw, the corporation that produced it. His investigations would give rise to his "Octopus" thesis.

A maid found Casolaro's body in a West Virginia hotel room on August 10, 1991. An unconvincing suicide note was found by his side. The slashes in Casolaro's wrists appeared too deep to be considered self-inflicted, and an accordion file of his most important research, which he kept with him at all times, has never been recovered. The night before he died, he met with a contact who would have made his Octopus thesis complete. On that night he called family and friends and warned them to be suspicious if an accident should befall him.So what was the substance of Casolaro's discovery, and could it really have led to his death?

Casolaro began his work with an investigation of Frank Nugan, co-founder of an Australian bank Nugan Hand, which went bankrupt in suspicious circumstances in 1980. Nugan was found shot dead in his car in Lithgow, Australia. In his pockets were lists recording the transfer of large amounts of money, and a business card of former CIA head, William Colby. Nugan's death came shortly after his partner, Michael Hand, announced that their bank could no longer pay its depositors, and that even its secured bonds were phony and valueless.

Casolaro's investigation of the collapsed bank revealed a massive money-laundering operation, linked both to narcotics trafficking and funding for the U.S. Military's Pine Gap satellite tracking station in Australia. Casolaro followed the trail of money transfers to Southeast Asia, where he encountered John Singlaub, the man who introduced him to PROMIS.

Singlaub had been involved in Operation Phoenix, which used an early version of PROMIS to track Viet Cong members. He was also involved with Air America, which ran weapons to the Vietnamese in exchange for heroin (see Alfred

In June 2003, Paul Redmond, Assistant Secretary for Information Analysis at the U.S. Homeland Security Department, resigned after discovering that Bin Laden possessed PROMIS, as reported by English investigative journalist Gordon Thomas. A legendary spy-catcher, responsible for the capture of FBI double-agent Aldrich Ames, among others, Redmond quit his post "for health reasons," although the generally accepted explanation for his departure was his frequently expressed frustration at the underfunding of his department. However, reporter Thomas claimed Redmond's resignation was precipitated by a secret investigation he had conducted into the Bin Laden/PROMIS link. Thomas concluded that Redmond had discovered long-standing common interests between the Bin Laden family and that of George W. Bush, and that it was the president himself who had forced Redmond to resign rather than reveal his discoveries.

Despite this attempted cover-up, it is increasingly believed that Bin Laden is using the U.S. government's own intelligence against them to escape capture and plot future attacks. This revelation—shocking if true—has its history in the research of Danny Casolaro. He discovered early, incautious uses of the PROMIS software as a bargaining chip by members of the American establishment, and his attempts to bring these bargains to light may have cost him his life.

Below: Journalist Danny Casolaro's body was found in hotel bathtub. after he had conducted a lengthy investigation into his "Octopus" theory.

McCoy's *The Politics of Heroin in Southeast Asia*). It seems likely that he sparked Casolaro's interest in PROMIS and the network of secrets that it increasingly attracted.

The final piece of the puzzle came when a reporter from New York's weekly newspaper *Village Voice* put Casolaro on to a story of a series of murders on the land of a native American tribe known as the Cabazons, outside Indio, California. The land was being used by a private security force called Wackenhut, specializing in information-gathering, which had built a weapons and research plant there. A number of tribal members protesting Wackenhut's presence on their land had been found murdered. In this investigation, Casolaro met his "Danger Man" Michael Riconosciuto (see page 82), who revealed to him the links between PROMIS and other scandals including the October Surprise and the Iran-Contra affair. The Octopus theory was born.

Less than a year after meeting Riconosciuto, and with his writing on the conspiracy incomplete, Danny was found dead.

CONSPIRACY LINKS:

PROMIS and the Internet

By the start of President Clinton's administration in 1993, posthumous distribution of Danny Casolaro's research had exposed the potential for PROMIS to be used in conjunction with the global Internet to collect data on private individuals anywhere in the world.

PROMIS software was requisitioned from Inslaw by cronies of former Attorney General Ed Meese, who served under Ronald Reagan. From here, it was illegally introduced into global banking network systems, where it allowed its sellers to spy on their clients by a "back-door"–a security breach set up by and only accessible to the creators of the software.

An early example of the potential dangers of this came in the death of Vince Foster, a White House aide found dead from a gunshot wound in Fort Marcy Park, northern Virginia on July 20, 1993. According to one theory, details of Vince Foster's Swiss bank accounts were made vulnerable by the PROMIS back door, and threatened revelations about their contents may have led to his suicide or even murder.

Above: PROMIS was hacked into through a "back door."

Spying on personal computers

Of most interest to the conspiracy student, however, was the ongoing development of PROMIS to spy on personal computer users. A discredited rumor had it that, when the original version of Windows 95 appeared, it contained a "back door" that surreptitiously read the user's hard drive and reported it back to Bill Gates. While this particular suggestion has since been discounted, the potential for a piece of software to report back on its user's data across the Internet is very real.

Encryption security and the Clipper chip–a "front door" strategy for keeping tabs on Internet use–remain important issues with the general public. Hacker Philip Zimmerman used a public domain algorithm to create the *Pretty Good Privacy* encryption software in 1991, and publicized it freely, bringing protection from computer hacking to the masses. However, PROMIS-like back doors continue to sneak onto the cyberscape. The espionage, security, and plain old marketing applications of back door access are sufficiently valuable that the problem will not go away. Business managers today even claim the right to spy on their employees' e-mail.

In January 2000, for example, a "glitch" in the protocol for removing phone listings from the website of *Yahoo!* made users' private address listings freely available to anyone punching in their phone number. Glitches were found in the Netscape browser in the mid-1990s that allowed the history of a user's session to be extracted, and supposedly secure operations to be decrypted. A bounty hunter group won US$1,000 from Netscape for locating the two young hackers responsible, one in Australia and the other in San Francisco. Two years later Netscape awarded another US$1,000 to a Danish software company called Cabocomm when it discovered another glitch, which allowed website operators to read anything stored on the hard-drive of a computer logged on to their site.

As Casolaro was well aware, knowledge is power, and protection of knowledge across the Internet is a major concern. The potential of the PROMIS system to collect personal, official, or military data from across the Internet lies at the heart of modern theorists' fears concerning the Octopus conspiracy.

How "back door" hacking works

A "back door" is simply a means for a programmer to circumvent security measures such as password protection that owners or users of the software may put in place. Daniel Brandt, who operates a web search engine named NameBase, argues that it is easy for any programmer to build such a security breach into any program they create, and that a system like PROMIS could take advantage. With physical access to any one computer, he says, " . . . PROMIS . . . can suck in every other database on earth, such as those used by utility companies, and correlate everything automatically."

Bill Hamilton, owner of Inslaw, the company that originally developed PROMIS, maintained that the program could run on almost any machine, and that the source code allowing further development and modification of the software, replete with the Inslaw name throughout the code commentary, was kept by any government that bought it. Casolaro believed that the U.S. government distributed PROMIS to intelligence agencies in other countries, with a back door allowing U.S. intelligence agencies access to the buyers' data.

Off-line hacking

Writer J. Orlin Grabbe explains how this process might work even on a closed system not connected to the Internet, "Since intelligence computers are, for security reasons, usually not connected to external networks, the original "back door" was a broadcast signal. The PROMIS software was often sold in connection with computer hardware (such as a Prime computer) using a specialized chip. The chip would broadcast the contents of the existing database to monitoring vans of collection satellites using digital spread spectrum techniques whenever the software was run. "

PROMIS and computer screens

Further information came to Casolaro from conversations with Michael Riconosciuto, who explained how PROMIS also used a process known as Van Eck hacking to access data on off-line computers.

Dutch scientist Wim Van Eck published an article in *Computers and Security* in December 1985, in which he outlined a system he had developed since January 1983 called "Van Eck" or "Tempest" phreaking. Computer monitors emit a faint radiation signal as they construct an image on screen. Van Eck was able to eavesdrop on this radiation, scan the information it contained, and use it to reconstruct the image on screen over a substantial distance on a modified television set. He used only readily available equipment, including a directional antenna, an antenna amplifier, a variable oscillator, and a frequency divider. The technique became popular for industrial espionage and has reportedly been used by various United States' government agencies.

According to Casolaro, Riconosciuto was familiar with Van Eck's techniques, and had seen them in action as part of PROMIS information gathering. Casolaro quotes Riconosciuto as saying, "An active phased array antenna is superfluous at the short distances he describes. A high performance surveillance receiver such as those made for Vatkins Johnson Corporation, Stoddarts/Singer or Fairchild will do the job quite nicely with a standard Biconical antenna...Brandt will find that if an arbitrarily small section of a sine function is known, the function is known everywhere."

Although Riconosciuto's claims are several levels above the average person's technical knowledge, Casolaro was convinced by his assurances that PROMIS could be used to monitor and report back on any computer, whether or not it was connected to a wider network, and that in theory it allowed its owners therefore to spy on any computer user on the planet.

It is surely the duty of any government in possession of this software to keep it out of the wrong hands. Yet Casolaro's investigations went on to reveal a dangerous complacency on the part of the U.S. administration when it came to distribution of this software.

PROMIS Sold!

Among other things, Casolaro wrote for a number of computer trade journals, and through his technical knowledge and meetings with informants such as Michael Riconosciuto and Jeff Steinberg, he became aware of a connection between Inslaw's remarkable software, PROMIS, and the October Surprise of the 1980 U.S. presidential campaigns.

Above: The first group of U.S. Embassy staffers in Tehran holds a press conference the day after Ayatollah Khomeini ordered their release.

In 1980, a deal was struck between members of Ronald Reagan's campaign team and Ayatollah Khomeini of Iran, to have Khomeini's followers retain 52 American hostages held at the U.S. Embassy in Teheran until Jimmy Carter had lost his presidential campaign. Casolaro learned that the October Surprise had cost the United States a US$40 million pay-off to the Ayatollah for the service.

Proof of the pay-off came when the past of Reagan's successor as president, George Bush Senior, was investigated. According to a 1963 memorandum released by the Assassinations Material Review Board (the government board created to declassify documents related to the JFK assassination), Bush claimed he had not worked for the CIA prior to his appointment as its director in 1976. But conspiracy theorists point to documentation that George Bush was

POINTS TO PONDER: ECHELON

- Another application of PROMIS involved the ECHELON satellite system, one of the components of the American Strategic Defense Initiative, or "Star Wars," designed to shoot down incoming ballistic missiles.
- ECHELON is a network of giant radar domes (radomes), satellite dishes, satellites, and networked super-computers originally designed to monitor satellite activity and give early warning of a potential missile launch anywhere in the globe.
- However, it is increasingly suspected that the real application of ECHELON is to use data gathered by satellite and from the airwaves to intercept and analyze virtually all phone and Internet communication across the globe.
- ECHELON satellite systems are renowned for their ability to take high-resolution photographs of objects as small as automobile license plates from high orbit, using "fusion framing," a permutation of the PROMIS software that can extrapolate visual information from pixellated photography taken over extremely long range.
- Casolaro's interest in ECHELON was raised by a series of deaths from 1982 to 1988 among scientists working for an S.D.I. (Strategic Defense Initiative) contractor named Marconi. Some 20 experts in super-computers and computer-controlled aircraft either could not control a car enough to avoid fatal accidents, or were so depressed by their highly paid professional success that they committed suicide.
- Casolaro feared that the combination of ECHELON's capabilities for gathering data from satellites and telecommunications with the access to computer records and data-tracking functions provided by PROMIS, could in theory be used to achieve total data control—possibly the ultimate aim of the Octopus network.
- More recently, ECHELON has been linked to the deaths of a number of microbiologists across the globe, including Don Wiley in Memphis Tennessee, and Victor Pasechnik, a Soviet defector resident in the United Kingdom. Pasechnik was debriefed by Dr. David Kelly, a U.K. weapons expert apparently driven to suicide after controversy surrounding the Iraq War and weapons of mass destruction. Is it possible that ECHELON was involved in his death?

receiving CIA debriefings as far back as the Kennedy assassination. He was also on hand in 1980 at a meeting in Paris for secret negotiations with the Iranians, according to the pilot who claims to have flown him there, Gunther Russbacher. In C.D. Stelzer's book *The Secret Life of Gunther Russbacher,* he asserts:

"As an aviator attached to the Office of Naval Intelligence, Russbacher says he piloted a BAC-111 aircraft—with George Bush on board—to Paris in 1980. Perhaps more importantly, Russbacher claims to have shuttled Bush back to the United States a few hours

Above: The radar domes of the top-secret joint U.S.-Australian missile defense base at Pine Gap, near Alice Springs in central Australia. Domes like these allow the ECHELON system to monitor global communications.

later in an SR-71 spy plane—and he professes to have proof. His knowledge of these events is the real reason he is in prison, Russbacher says."

Bush's French rendezvous purportedly finalized earlier negotiations between the Reagan-Bush campaign and Islamic revolutionaries. It was at these talks that the delayed release of the 52 American hostages was allegedly negotiated, and at this meeting the US$40 million up front cash payment was allegedly agreed.

Casolaro asserted that Ayatollah Khomeini received the money from the Attorney General, Edwin Meese, through Earl Brian, an associate of Ronald Reagan. Casolaro claimed that, as a reward for this service, Brian was put in charge of the sale of the PROMIS software, to negotiate as he pleased. Brian promptly sold PROMIS to the CIA, MI5, MI6, Interpol, the Mossad, and the Royal Canadian Mounted Police—even though the software was in fact the property of Inslaw, and selling it was a criminal act.

Casolaro believed he had discovered that, far from protecting the PROMIS system for the security of its citizens, the U.S. government had instead cynically sold it in politically dubious circumstances to other governments worldwide. Casolaro's outrage was only to increase when he learned of the uses to which funds from the illegal sale of the software were put.

> "Russbacher claims to have shuttled Bush back to the United States a few hours later in an SR-71 spy plane and he professes to have proof. His knowledge of these events is the real reason he is in prison, Russbacher says."

The Iran-Contra affair
By the end of the Reagan years and the beginning of the Bush administration, Casolaro believed he had uncovered a link between proceeds from the sale of PROMIS, and the Iran-Contra affair that led to political scandal and criminal prosecutions in the late 1980s.

In 1986, it emerged that prominent members of the Reagan administration had been involved in the secret sale of arms to Iran, an avowed enemy of the United States, in violation both of U.S. government policy and the Arms Export Control Act. Moreover, funds from these sales had been used to aid a right-wing terrorist and drug-trafficking group in Nicaragua known as the Contras, in an effort to destabilize the democratic but leftist Nicaraguan government. (See page 56 for more details.)

Casolaro claimed to have discovered that the hostage negotiations and funds from the sale of PROMIS were a springboard for the arms sales, and that many of the key players in the October Surprise, the sale of PROMIS, and the Iran-Contra affair were the same. To Casolaro, by this stage, it was thus apparent that a team of former covert intelligence operatives, in the highest echelons of the United States government, had established an international network of gun- and drug-trafficking, and money laundering. This team was the entity that Casolaro named "Octopus," and as his research continued, its members' pursuit of personal power led the group into increasingly large-scale political scandals and war.

"Danger Man"
Casolaro's guide to the connections between these controversies was a man named Michael Riconosciuto. A child prodigy, who at age 14 had gone to work as an assistant to a Nobel prize-winning physicist, Riconosciuto would become Danny Casolaro's chief informant and provide the basis for his unfinished Octopus book. Casolaro called Riconosciuto "Danger Man" because of the world of

shadowy intrigue he occupied. At the time of their meeting, Riconosciuto worked for a private security and data-tracking firm called Wackenhut, which owned an illegal copy of PROMIS supposedly obtained through Octopus. Riconosciuto was employed to figure out ways of improving PROMIS, using its millions of lines of code to spread the power and control of Wackenhut's clients.

Shortly before he met Casolaro, Riconosciuto had declared in legal affidavits that he worked at the behest of Earl Brian—who arranged the sale of PROMIS—to modify the software. It was Riconosciuto who outfitted it with the back door capability, and the predictive function that Osama Bin Laden may have found so useful in later years. Ironically, when coded with Riconosciuto's modifications, PROMIS not only tracked and extrapolated the activities of criminals to report back to its users, it also collected data on the users to report back to the people who sold it in the first place. By this means, Octopus could spy on all the agencies to which it had illegally sold PROMIS, including the Royal Canadian Mounted Police, Interpol, the Mossad, and the CIA.

“Wackenhut owned an illegal copy of PROMIS and was trying to figure out ways of improving it, using its millions of lines of code to spread the power and control of its clients.”

As part of his employment by Octopus, Riconosciuto also claims to have met Osama Bin Laden in the late 1980s, during CIA negotiations with the Mujahadeen, and to have attempted to sell Bin Laden shoulder-firing Man Portable Air Defense Systems (MANPADS), the missile launchers used against American troops in the most recent Afghanistan War.

Riconosciuto's pedigree as a covert agent could be traced back to Fred Crisman, a close business associate of Riconosciuto's father. Crisman was a veteran of World War II and was reactivated for service in the Korean War. In between, however, he primarily became known for his connection to the Maury Island UFO event in 1947 near Tacoma, Washington. Prosecuting Attorney Jim Garrison subpoenaed Fred Crisman as part of his investigation of J.F.K.'s death in 1968. For Casolaro, these connections all confirmed his suspicions that a very small group of people were behind a great number of political controversies in post-War America. Sadly, Casolaro died before he could bring his story to the world.

DARPA and Octopus today

Despite Casolaro's death, evidence still continues that Octopus continues to operate. In 2002, George Bush Junior appointed Poindexter, newly pardoned for his crimes during the Iran-Contra

Above: Shoulder-launched missile launcher being fired. These weapons avoid the problem of recoil by directing all exhaust out the rear of the launch tube. They were used against U.S. troops in the war in Afghanistan and were allegedly sold to the enemy by the Americans.

affair, as head of a new information technology unit of DARPA, the Defense Advanced Research Projects Agency. Dubbed Total Information Awareness (TIA), the new office depicted itself with the symbol of an eye over a pyramid, a symbol instantly recognizable to conspiracy theorists across the globe. TIA declared its purpose to be "developing computer software that could virtually track every detail of an individual's life," software that sounds very much like a version of PROMIS. Poindexter was forced to resign from the Bush administration when Reuters reported that he planned to profit from a futures trading market based on the prediction of terrorist events.

Two conspiracy researchers, Tom Flocco and Michael Ruppert, later investigated the use of PROMIS data-gathering to profit from insider trading deals. In pursuing their story, Ruppert and Flocco got the first ever confession from an official CIA spokesperson, that the CIA used PROMIS, ". . . beyond American borders, to scrutinize world financial markets for national security purposes." The covert quest for total data control continues.

The story told by Casolaro, and its continuation to today's struggles, is one of greed, power-lust, and manipulation. And, with the use of PROMIS still shrouded in secrecy, many people fear that its consequences for global security have not yet become apparent.

DC Snipers

During the fall of 2002, beginning on September 14, Washington DC was held in scope of a .223 caliber rifle borne by an unknown sniper. The terror lasted for 23 days, with the apparently random shootings of 13 people, of whom ten died.

Right: The M40, a military standard-issue sniper rifle.

By October 22, DC authorities arrested two suspects: John Allen Muhammad, 41, and John Lee Malvo, 17. The many twists and turns in the police investigation were played out on live television, with regular news conferences given by the Montgomery County Police Chief Charles Moose to an increasingly anxious public. The capture of the two suspects resulted not so much from good detective work as from a trail of messages left by the suspects themselves, including phone calls, voicemail messages, cryptic notes, and Tarot cards, that showed a marked intention to themselves to the authorities.

The death of Ken Bridges

Notably absent from the story as it unfolded were any details concerning the victims and the sites of the shootings, and perhaps more importantly, information regarding the motivation behind the killings.

One of victims the snipers killed on October 11 was Ken Bridges, an important figure among African-Americans for his involvement in the initial phases of the direct marketing program POWER (People Organized and Working for Economic Rebirth). POWER was conceived in 1986 by Minister Louis Farrakhan, head of the Nation of Islam, a separatist religious socio-political organization. Farrakhan had

"Ken Bridges, an important figure among African-Americans for his involvement in the initial phases of the direct marketing program POWER."

selected Bridges as the program's national spokesman, and to serve as its Vice President.

The Nation of Islam Connection

In the weeks that followed the arrests, other connections between the killings and the Nation of Islam came to light, casting doubt on the official description of the shootings as a randon rampage. Speculation mounted that Muhammad, one of the snipers, had worked as a security operative for the Nation of Islam, for example, at the Million Man March, a march of protest and unity convened by the Nation of Islam in Washington DC on October 16, 1995. The event had been held to try to increase black involvement in community activism. On October 25, 2002, Louis Farrakhan held a news conference in response to speculation. Although he had organized the march, Farrakhan denied that he had provided security for it, but he did acknowledge that suspected sniper John Allen Muhammad had belonged to the Nation of Islam.

Below: Sniper suspect Malvo is brought into court to be identified by a witness during the murder trial.

Media Interference

On October 25, 2002, with speculation surrounding the shootings at its height, Minnesota senator Paul Wellstone was killed when his campaign plane crashed in northern Minnesota. The *St. Petersburg Times* reporter Eric Deggans commented on the media attention focused on the two separate cases, "Even as the story wound down Friday morning, the punditry continued. Fox News Channel anchor Bridget Quinn quizzed a forensic scientist on the possibility that Muhammad was an adherent of Nation of Islam leader Louis Farrakhan. Hours later, news of Minnesota Sen. Paul Wellstone's death pushed such coverage aside, at least for a while, offering hope that a better news balance would return soon."

"The curious connections emerging between the DC sniper case and the Nation of Islam fell from the media radar."

The media focus shifted to the death of the senator and the election of Wellstone's replacement, former Vice President Walter Mondale. The curious connections emerging between the DC sniper case and the Nation of Islam fell from the media radar, leaving the African-American community to mourn the loss of Ken Bridges, and many questions about the death of this iconic figure unanswered.

PEOPLE IN PURSUIT:

Loren Coleman

Loren Coleman is a prolific writer with 27 published titles to his name. His most recent book, *The Copycat Effect: How the Media and Popular Culture Trigger the Mayhem in Tomorrow's Headlines*, examines the media's propensity to ignore the conspiratorial context of current events, including those surrounding the arrest of the DC snipers.

He also has a reputation as one of the world's leading authorities on unexplained and paranormal phenomena. He began such investigations in 1958, after encountering the work of Charles Fort, an author famous for spending his life scanning periodical articles in the New York public library and the British Museum collecting notes on phenomena that lay outside accepted theories and beliefs of the time to demonstrate that official science covered up as much as it discovered. Coleman expanded his approach to the "Fortean" in 1960 to include cryptozoology, the study of unknown and legendary animals.

By 1969, Coleman started sharing his experiences of such global mysteries in print and on television. His bestsellers included a cult classic called *Mysterious America* and a biography on Texas oil millionaire Tom Slick entitled *Tom Slick and the Search for the Yeti*. Slick led several major expeditions to the Himalayas between 1956 and 1959, ostensibly in search of the Yeti, but perhaps also providing cover for CIA attempts to sneak the Dalai Lama out of Tibet. Coleman also covered Slick's pursuit of Bigfoot in the Pacific Northwest in *Bigfoot! The True Story of Apes in America*, published in 2003.

Coleman appeared frequently on radio and television programs, and has lectured throughout North America, as well as in London and at Loch Ness. He has been both on- and off-camera consultant to reality-based programs including

There was a general sense that the connections were never satisfactorily explored. In his October 26 piece in *The Black World Today*, journalist Herb Boyd wrote:

"It comes as no surprise that MSNBC trotted out Brian Levin on Friday morning to draw some wild association between John Allen Muhammad, the man arrested in the sniper case, and the Nation of Islam. Levin, a former NYPD officer and now a criminologist who teaches at California State University at San Bernardino, asserted that Muhammad didn't fit the profile of the usual sniper, but he did possess other characteristics that might have been crucial to such behavior. As a believer in a regimented theology . . . with all sorts of strict discipline, such sociopathic behavior was not uncommon. He took pains to distinguish the Nation of Islam from orthodox Islam, noting its anti-American sentiments, its desire to separate from mainstream America and its hatred of whites."

Boyd concluded: "The mainstream media's competitive rush to get the news is too often not accompanied by accuracy or fact checking, and to march out so-called experts like Levin with an agenda and an ax to grind only compounds the spread of misinformation."

UNN theory

Members of Ital Iman I's Underground News Network—an African-American activist journal—took an entirely different spin on the events. They saw hidden messages in the actions of the snipers.

NBC-TV's *Unsolved Mysteries*, A & E's *Ancient Mysteries*, the History Channel's *In Search of History*, and the Discovery Channel's *In the Unknown*. He has contributed regular columns to the UK-based magazine *Fortean Times*, and to *Fate*, the digest magazine of paranormal reporting in the United States.

Coleman majored in anthropology at Southern Illinois University-Carbondale. He received a graduate degree in psychiatric social work from Simmons College in Boston in 1978, and was admitted to two PhD programs, taking doctoral coursework in anthropology at Brandies University, and in sociology at the University of New Hampshire.

As a sociologist, Coleman gained acclaim with his book, *Suicide Clusters*. Coleman enjoyed a second career in the national media discussing causal links between seemingly unrelated suicides. His work on the suicides of baseball players, specifically Angels' pitcher Donnie Moore, received wide attention and acclaim.

His work has involved training and the creation of manuals for law enforcement officers on forensic guidelines in child abuse and suicide investigations, and dealing with the media. Since the 1980s, Coleman has trained and consulted across the United States and Canada on unexplained phenomena, cryptozoology, media affairs, suicide clusters, and school violence.

As a professor at New England universities, Coleman became the first to offer a course in cryptozoology, and continues working with institutions such as Oberlin College and Florida Keys Community College-Pangea Institute, on new offerings in this field. From 1983 to 1996 he served as a senior research associate at the Edmund S. Muskie School of Public Policy.

Above: The tarot card for Death, left for the police.

Natalie Hopkinson of *The Washington Post* observed that the UNN "saw significance in the four gas stations targeted by the snipers [which] represented the four big oil companies. The tarot card left for police was the 13th card of the deck corresponding to death, and it alluded to the 13-year-old boy shot at the school as a warning to the government that schools should be places of learning. The numerical links he makes go on and on."

But the supposed hidden messages had far greater implications relating to the economic empowerment of African-Americans. Hopkinson goes on to note: "Soon after the UNN began publishing its trial coverage, criticism came from the Matah Network of Ken Bridges, who was shot in the back by the sniper at an Exxon station in Spotsylvania County. Some Matah advocates regard Bridges as a 'modern-day Marcus Garvey.'" (Garvey was an important proponent of the 1920s' Back-to-Africa movement, who died before he could carry out his work of "economically empowering black America"). The Matah supporters believed Muhammad was coerced by the government to kill Bridges in a conspiracy that would stifle black economic power.

The problem of whom to believe

Some critics took a more balanced approach. Loren Coleman, for example, who examined media response to the DC snipers case in his book *The Copycat Effect*, observed: "One is left not knowing what to believe in the DC snipers case, and that's the problem. Or perhaps, that's the plan. Too much of the so-called mainstream media was spending time on sensationally spinning the terrorism angle in the story and not looking deeply. The radical African-American press was pointing at conspiracy theories and lines of connections pro- or con-Nation of Islam. In the end, responsible journalism was not served well by how the story unfolded in the local or national media."

"The four gas stations targeted by the snipers represented the four big oil companies . . . The numerical links . . . go on and on."

The Washington DC sniper case demonstrates the many faceted issues that stem from massive media attention to what Coleman calls a "hot death story." The

POINTS TO PONDER: NATION OF ISLAM

- Muhammad had joined the Nation of Islam in 1997, and unconfirmed reports circulated that he had previously belonged to the Five Percent Nation, a loosely knit religious group which split from the Nation of Islam in 1964.
- Open warfare exists between members the Five Percenters and the Nation of Islam held in the prison system.
- Links between the snipers and the Nation of Islam fell out of the news within two days. The media quickly lost interest in the question of whether or not John Allen Muhammad had worked as a bodyguard for the Nation of Islam.
- The fact that Muhammad bought a US$800 Bushmaster rifle, a computer, communications gear, a car, and flew around the country claiming he worked as an operative for the CIA and FBI also went unreported.
- Did political correctness cause the media to back away from the Nation of Islam connection, and drift instead toward the often-used "lone gunman" theory?
- Victim Ken Bridges was a member of the Amway Corporation, and co-founder of the Matah Network, an Afrocentric marketing network, with the black leader, Representative David P. Richardson, Jr.
- Richardson was an outspoken critic of the police. He died suddenly, a week prior to the formal opening of the 1995 Congressional hearings on Operation Fruehmenschen, an FBI project to prosecute black political leaders.

media reports an important news event before the full facts are known, other than in terms of death and mayhem. The lurid aspects of the story assume a dominant place in the headlines, reportage, and nightly overviews of world events, pushing aside any background elements that get in the way of pure titillation. Reporters perform little analysis of deeper issues that might prevent future tragedy, and practically no investigation of the actual events, relying instead on press conferences and official pronouncements. They present arrests or conclusions as a breaking story, and ignore avenues of inquiry about possible conspiracies behind them. Looking too deeply into motives and links is often left to the alternative media to explore, where it can be quickly dismissed as crazy conspiracy theories.

9/11 and the order to intercept

Just as every American knows where he or she was on hearing about Kennedy's assassination, so too will every American remember September 11, 2001, when planes crashed into New York's World Trade Center, the Pentagon, and in a field near Shanksville, Pennsylvania.

Right: The Twin Towers following the collision of the two airplanes.

Decades may pass before all the conspiracy theories have been considered over the tragic events of September 11, 2001, let alone answers found to the many questions that still surround them. Or perhaps not: it took three years from the time of Kennedy's assassination until the first major conspiracy books about it appeared, whereas, by September 12, 2001, conspiracy writer Robin Ramsay had saved 3.1 megabytes of computer files on the 9/11 attacks.

In his magazine *Lobster* Ramsay reports that, "[This] was the first mega event in the Internet age . . . and that culture's response was very striking. Within hours all manner of people with different political positions, mostly but not exclusively from the United States, had decided—had assumed—that the event was phony; a stunt. They knew, they could see, they could intuit (since there was almost no evidence to work with) that this was a stunt by—majority view—the U.S. state." According to a Zogby Poll taken in August 2004, 49.3 percent of New York City residents, believe that the U.S. government might have been involved in the attacks.

An uncertain chain of events

One theory that implicated the U.S. government involved President Bush's orders to shoot down the hijacked planes. Had George Bush given an order to shoot down the hijacked planes and, if so, did he do it in time? Vice President Dick Cheney told congressional investigators that Bush did give such an order. Pilots who flew that day, however, contradict him.

As the man running the White House emergency center, Cheney claims that Bush authorized the shooting down of commercial aircraft shortly after finishing his well-known reading of *The Pet Goat* for children at Emma E. Booker Elementary School in Sarasota, Florida. Transportation Secretary Norman Mineta backed up this claim in testimony before the U.S. congressional committee investigating the tragedies. Mineta testified that he was in Cheney's presence when an aide came in with reports that the plane headed for the Pentagon "is 50 miles out. . . the plane is 30 miles out. . ." As the gap closed to ten miles, Mineta testified that the young man asked, "Do the orders still stand?" According to Mineta, Cheney replied, "Of course the orders still stand. Have you heard anything to the contrary?" Yet a number of organizations dispute this.

Above: FBI agents, fire fighters, rescue workers, and engineers work at the Pentagon crash site on September 14, 2001, where a hijacked American Airlines flight slammed into the building on 9/11. The terrorist attack caused extensive damage to the west face of the building.

9/11 CitizensWatch theory

The 9/11 CitizensWatch is one such group. They launched an advertising campaign that ran concurrently with the congressional 9/11 hearings. They declared in newspaper advertisements and subway posters that there was a possibility of some kind of cover-up: any plane that loses its transponder signal—as the hijacked planes had—has jets scrambled to intercept it as a matter of standard procedure. So why had this not happened on 9/11?

At his previous Senate confirmation hearing, two days after 9/11, Joint Chiefs Chairman Richard Myers had testified that fighters were not scrambled until after the American Airlines Flight 77 flew into the Pentagon at around 9:37 AM. Why so late, when it was obvious that a dramatic turn in its flight plan had occurred at 9 AM? The North American Aerospace Defense Command (NORAD) asserted also that it did not scramble jets until after the attack on the Pentagon. Even if this were true, however, NORAD's intercepts still had time to reach at least two of the other three flights. Additionally, the flight that hit the Pentagon could have been downed by surface-to-air missiles at the White House had Vice President Cheney given the go ahead.

Over two years after the attacks, Myers and Defense Secretary Donald Rumsfeld told the same congressional investigation that they still did not know why the military failed to respond. Only three months before 9/11 the Joint Chiefs had amended the standing directive used by operational commanders regarding a "request for destruction of derelict airborne objects" in which potentially lethal support requires the approval of the Secretary of Defense. This made Rumsfeld responsible for a shoot-down order,

PEOPLE IN PURSUIT:

Thierry Meyssan

French author Thierry Meyssan (*L'Effroyable Imposture* (*The Frightening Fraud*) and *Pentagate*) has suggested that a plane did not hit the Pentagon at all on 9/11. Rather, that damage to the building was caused by an unmanned drone aircraft or a cruise missile. The popularity of this theory provides some measure of the extent to which George W. Bush has become a conspiracy-laden president.

Some who reject Meyssan's idea do accept the notion of Bush's culpability for 9/11. Most moderate 9/11 conspiracy theories, including Len Bracken's *The Shadow Government: 9/11 and State Terror* (AUP, 2002), hold the proposition that the Bush Administration allowed 9/11 to happen as part of a political strategy to take advantage of terrorist incidents and rule by a tension turned into a global war on terror.

They find support for this in Bush's lingering in a Florida elementary school after receiving the report of the 9/11 attacks. Vice President Dick Cheney told Congressional investigators that shortly afterward Bush gave the order to shoot down any commercial aircraft being used as part of the attack–an order given in time to stop the Pentagon-bound Flight 77. Military pilots said they did not receive such an order.

Observers described the 2004 United States elections as a choice between the lesser of two "Bonesmen." According to the Skull and Bones

yet he could not tell Congress with any certainty that such an order had been communicated to the pilots.

An unnamed Pentagon official, who was in charge of the command center and who co-ordinated a conference call between the White House, the Federal Aviation Administration (FAA), and NORAD, testified to Congress that the lack of intercept had to do with the assumption that the four hijackings were unrelated. Yet, under normal procedure, jets should have scrambled after them, related or not.

Above: Director of Federal Facilities Division, giving a briefing at the Pentagon on damages sustained after American Airlines Flight 77 crashed into the Pentagon.

fraternity membership list (www.biblebelievers.org.au/bones.htm) both major candidates belonged to the secret fraternity Skull & Bones when at Yale University. The suspicions aroused by George W. Bush's administration have ruptured any remaining notions that conspiracy occurs only on rare occasions. The facts behind 9/11 and the ensuing wars remain clouded in conspiracy.

Right: Thierry Meyssan

Paranoid citizens

Critics suggest that the evidence now indicates that the orders discussed in Mineta's testimony refer to a "stand down" rather than a "shoot down" order. However, the truth of the matter may never be resolved. What is clear is that after 9/11, paranoia was no longer the exclusive province of conspiracy critics, but had spread to the everyday citizens of the United States as well.

Left: A New York City fire fighter looks up at what remains of the World Trade Center after its collapse.

Right: The cover of *Time* magazine shows a photograph of the World Trade Center's Twin Towers burning after terrorists crashed two commerical airplanes into the buildings.

POINTS TO PONDER:

- Pilots in the air that day have told researcher John Judge, who co-founded a group called 9/11 CitizensWatch, that the military's failure to act when the planes were known to have been hijacked suggest that the executive orders may have been to "stand down" rather than to "shoot down."
- One file collected by Ramsay in the aftermath of the attacks reflected the immediate suspicions raised at the website "www.whatreallyhappened.com." "Troubling questions arose about the alleged pilot-hijackers of the four aircraft, who were supposedly trained on Cessna aircraft over the past year at fields in Florida and Oklahoma. One general officer seriously questions whether these novices could have located a target dead-on 200 miles (320 kilometers) removed from takeoff point, much less controlled the flight and mastered the intricacies of instrument flight rules, and all accomplished in 45 minutes. The extremely skilful maneuvering of the three aircraft at near mach speeds, each unerringly hitting its target, was superb. As one Air Officer a veteran of over 100 sorties over North Vietnam—explained, 'Those birds [commercial airliners] either had a crack fighter pilot in the left seat, or they were being maneuvered by remote control'."

TIME
SEPTEMBER 11
2001

Polonium poison

"To thine own self be true."
(Polonius)

Late in 2006, former Russian spy and political dissident Alexander Litvinenko was killed using the rare radioactive poison Polonium-210. He is widely believed to have been silenced by the Russian government.

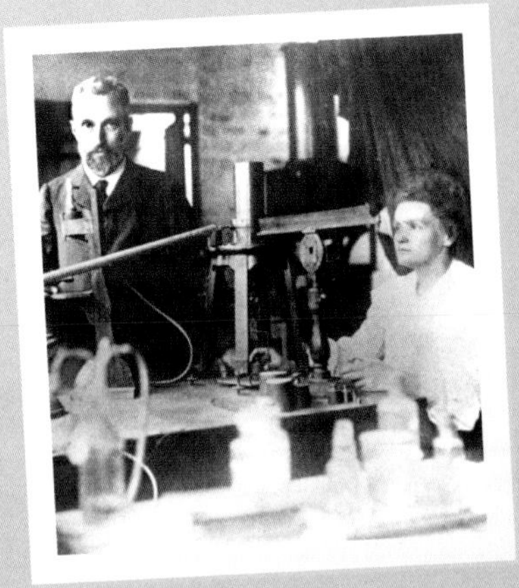

Right: Marie Curie working in a makeshift laboratory, rue Lhomond in Paris.

The name of the radioactive element Polonium-210 derives from the word Poland, the territory where its discoverer, Marie Curie, was born. In the late 1880s, Poland had no independence from Russia, a fact Madame Curie and her husband felt they could draw some public attention to by thus naming one of their discoveries. Perhaps their efforts were successful: Poland gained its sovereignty after World War I. Polonium, however, returned in the early twenty-first century as a deadly warning for those who, perhaps on the advice of Shakespeare's Polonius, defied oppressive Russia.

"once inside the body in even small amounts, it causes massive acute radiation poisoning."

The element itself is an extremely rare metal. It is highly radioactive in all its forms, releasing energetic alpha particles that cause the surrounding air to glow faintly, and generating enough heat that it has been used in some spacecraft to prevent freezing of internal components. Its high radioactivity makes it very rare in nature, so any significant amount must be synthesized at great expense. As a result, it is very rarely available outside specialist industrial or aeronautical processes. The alpha particles it produces cannot pass through skin, making it relatively harmless unless ingested, inhaled, or otherwise absorbed into the body. However, once inside the body in even small amounts, it causes massive acute radiation poisoning. Alpha particles released into the intestines and vital organs damage fragile cells, causing organ failure and death. The minumum lethal dose for an average human being is estimated to be about 50 nanograms (billionths of a

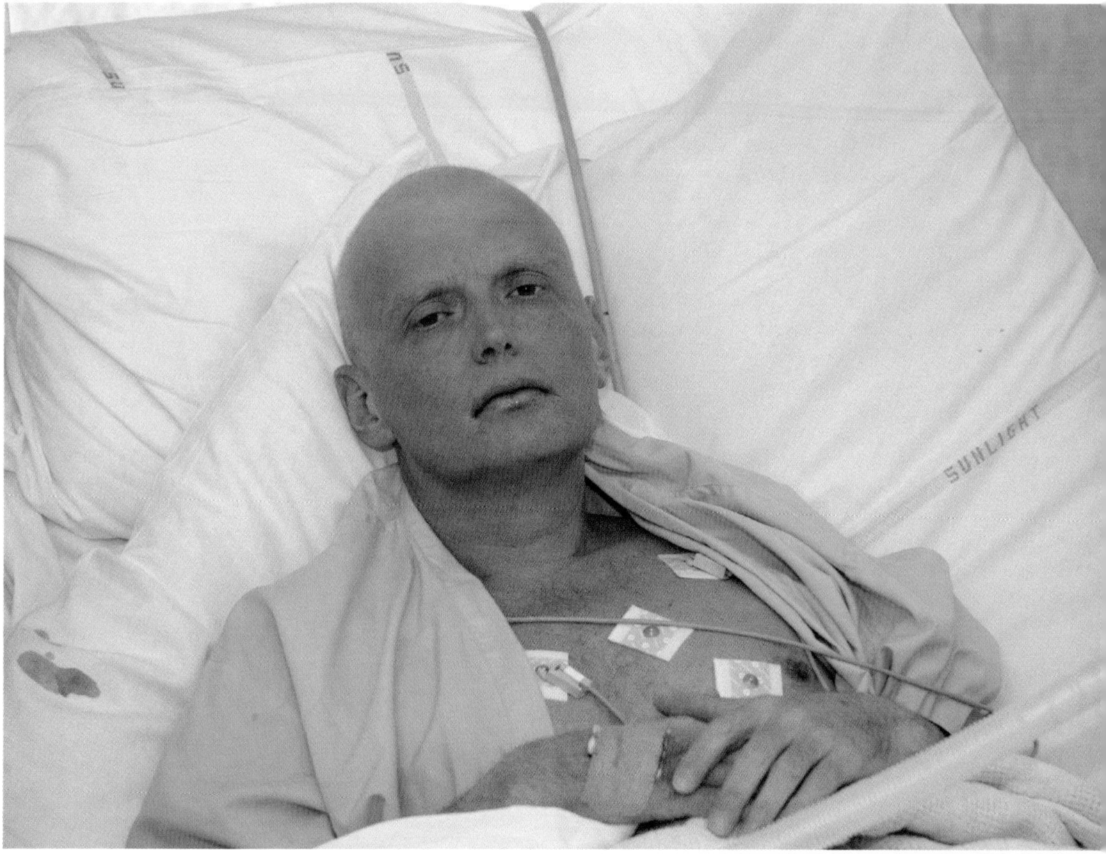

gram), although in practise-because radioactive decay takes place over time, an amount closer to 1 microgram (millionth of a gram) may be required.

In 2006 one man, former secret police agent Alexander Litvinenko, died from polonium poisoning. But was the Russian state behind his death? The answers lie in another conflict.

Above: Alexander Litvinenko at the Intensive Care Unit of University College Hospital on November 20, 2006 in London, England. The 43-year-old former KGB spy, who died on November 23, accused Russian President Vladimir Putin of involvement in his death.

Chechnya's struggle for independence

The territory struggling for its sovereignty in this case was Chechnya, north of the Caucasus Mountains and the Caspian Sea. The central event—from which a list of the suspicious deaths has followed—is an apartment complex bombing on September 13, 1999 that killed and wounded over 300 Chechen citizens. It was the latest in a series of bombing incidents that Vladimir Putin's government blamed on separatists and used as the pretext for a war to secure Russia's dominance of the province. Many in Russia saw this incident as a "false flag" operation masterminded by the Russian government to justify a military response.

Above: A picture of slain journalist Anna Politkovskaya is shown during a candlelight vigil in front of the Russian Embassy October 16, 2006 in Washington DC.

Anna Politkovskaya's assasssination

Anna Politkovskaya was among the most renowned journalists to decry the ongoing Russian military presence in Chechnya. In her newspaper columns for *Novaya Gazeta* and her books, *A Small Corner of Hell: Dispatches From Chechnya* and *Putin's Russia*, she detailed the abuse, murders, and torture that took place during the Chechen war, and was openly critical of both Putin and the Chechen government. When she was not busy meeting with informants, running from troops and interviewing the war's victims, she became the most visible and vocal critic on the topic. That criticism ended abruptly with her assassination on October 7, 2006, by gunshot at her apartment complex's elevator door.

Enter Alexander Litvinenko, one-time head of the KGB successor agency, the FSB. Perhaps the least of his accusations against the Putin government was that Putin himself had ordered Anna Politkovskaya's assassination. He had warned her to escape Russia as he himself had when he fled to the UK and asked for asylum on November 1, 2000. Litvinenko had been imprisoned in Russian jails after he allowed several top officers to come forward in 1999 with reports that they had been ordered to assassinate Russian businessman Boris Berezovsky and several others.

"he received warning from a former FSB agent that a special unit had been assigned to assassinate him in 2002."

Litvinenko's conspiracy theories

Litvinenko proved to be the ultimate conspiracy theorist of Russian affairs. His accusations against Putin's administration included the idea that the FSB had trained many Al-Qaeda terrorists, including Ayman al-Zawahiri, Osama Bin Laden's second-in-command. He maintained that Putin was behind the September 13, 1999 and attendant bombings, including an infamous hostage incident at a Moscow theater in 2002. Russian authorities confiscated thousands of copies of a book Litvinenko wrote on this topic. He accused Vladimir Putin of everything from involvement with organized crime to pedophilia. Litvinenko, also an EU member, alleged that Romano Prodi, later prime minister of Italy, worked for the KGB and suggested that he had a connection to the notorious Red Brigades assassination of Aldo Moro.

None of this endeared Litvinenko to the Russian state. In fact, he received warning from a former FSB agent that a special unit had been assigned to assassinate him in 2002. He nevertheless remained true to the spirit of Polonius, that is, true to himself and persisted with his criticism of Putin in exile for the next several years, maintaining that Putin had come to power via an F.S.B. coup and maintained it by force, through assassination, and by creating a fear of terrorism through the various "false flag" bombings attributed to Chechnyan separatists.

At lunchtime on November 1, 2006, Litvinenko met with an Italian friend and contact, Mario Scaramella, who had information on the killing of Anna Politkovskaya, at a sushi restaurant in London. By nightfall, Litvinenko was in hospital, poisoned with the infamous radioactive isotope.

Above: President Vladimir Putin, suspected by some of being behind the deaths of both Politkovskaya and Litvinenko.

By November 23, amid much media attention, Litvinenko was dead. His final written message defiantly held to the principles to which he had remained true, if only to underscore what his enemy and the man he suspected of masterminding his assassination, Vladimir Putin, had lacked: "You have shown yourself to be barbaric and ruthless as your most hostile critics have claimed. You have shown yourself to have no respect for life, liberty, or any civilized value. You have shown yourself to be unworthy of the trust of civilized men and women."

Theories surrounding Litvinenko's death

Litvinenko succumbed quickly to the massive dose of Polonium-210 he had ingested in the sushi restaurant. Previous cases of exposure had occurred in Marie Curie's daughter, and members of the scientific community in Israel who worked with it in the late 1950s to 60s, all of whom died from leukemia or other cancers that could not necessarily be tracked back to the single isotope. These other cases were matters of exposure; Litvinenko, however, had ingested the lethal substance. Toxicologist John Henry, a prominent figure in the investigation of the poisoning of Ukrainian president Viktor Yushenko, at first attributed the poisoning to thallium, but tests ultimately demonstrated the cause as the far rarer Polonium-210, found virtually exclusively in state-run nuclear reactors and radioisotope laboratories.

Panic ensued in London, as traces of the deadly substance were found in a trail across the city, and the authorities ran tests on all those who had come in contact with Litvinenko at the sushi bar. Radioactive traces were found in a dozen places in London and on two British Airways planes. Litvinenko's wife Mariana and his contact Mario Scaramella both tested positive for small doses of the substance but neither developed any symptoms of poisoning.

The theories moved in all directions, of course. Some suggested that Litvinenko, a Muslim, had actually been caught up in a terrorist attempt to smuggle nuclear materials. Others theorized that Litvinenko's death itself was a false flag operation carried out by Russia's Yukos oil barons to help alleviate legal problems brought on them by the Putin administration. The acting president of the Chechen republic claims to this day that the exile billionaire Boris Berezovsky had Litvinenko killed in order to weaken the Russian state.

"A message has been communicated to anyone who wants to speak out against the Kremlin: If you do, no matter who you are, where you are, we will find you, and we will silence you in the most horrible way possible."

Nothing concrete has so far come of the official investigation into Litvinenko's death. It remains officially unsolved and, in addition to fueling the "false flag" accusations of conspiracy theorists, has lead to a growing international suspicion in official circles that Russia has returned to the bad old days of KGB "rule-by-assassination." These suspicions arise not only from the list of suspicious deaths that preceded Litvinenko but also that apparently followed.

On February 26, 2007, Paul Joyal, an expert on Russia's covert intelligence world who had served as a staff member of the U.S. Select Senate Committee on Intelligence, alleged on the national TV broadcast Dateline NBC that Litvinenko's murder served as a signal by Putin's regime of what would become of its critics. True to his own conscience, and undeterred by possible threats against his own life, Joyal said to an NBC reporter: "A message has been communicated to anyone who wants to speak out against the Kremlin: If you do, no matter who you are, where you are, we will find you, and we will silence you in the most horrible way possible."

On Thursday, March 1, Joyal was shot by two men outside of his home in a normally peaceful DC suburb in Maryland. Joyal remains hospitalized in critical condition and, "officially," the incident has been attributed to a random crime.

Plame game

The Plame affair developed into the biggest political scandal of George W. Bush's presidency. Did members of the Bush administration really "out" a CIA covert operative? And has the role of senior government figures in the exposure been covered up?

Right: Dick Cheney refused to discuss his chief of staff's alleged involvement in the case on *Meet the Press*.

In 2003, the identity of CIA covert operative Valerie Plame was illegally leaked to the press, severely compromising her activities and, some say, putting her life in danger. More shocking still was the suggestion that the leak had come from senior members of the Bush administration. Political heavyweights were quick to distance

Right: Valerie Plame Wilson testifies before the House Oversight and Government Reform Committee on March 16, 2007, in Washington DC.

themselves from the scandal, and by February 2007, investigators were no nearer to identifying the source of the leak. Government aides had raised a smoke-screen of conflicting stories that may permanently conceal the truth.

One of these aides was Lewis "Scooter" Libby, chief of staff to Vice President Dick Cheney. Prosecutors officially charged Libby in 2006 with lying to and obstructing the investigation, and he was found guilty in 2007 on four of five charges. His conviction drew attention away from the original question of who had actually leaked Plame's identity. Has he been made a scapegoat for a much more senior figure responsible for the security breach? And why would any official wish to compromise the security of a CIA agent?

Below: "Scooter" Libby was found guilty of charges relating to obstruction and perjury in the investigation into the disclosure of Plame's identity.

An issue of WMD?

The answer may lie in Iraq. According to well-known television pundit Robert Novak, former Deputy Secretary of State Richard Armitage leaked Plame's identity in order to get back at her husband, former Ambassador Joseph Wilson. Wilson published a report in 2003, entitled "What I Didn't Find in Africa," stating that no evidence could be found for any attempt by Saddam Hussein to procure yellowcake uranium from Nigeria in the late 1990s—one of the prime arguments for the presence of weapons of mass destruction in Iraq.

This report, which appeared as a *New York Times* opinion piece, dealt a great blow to the Bush administration's arguments for the existence of WMD in pre-war Iraq. The waters were further muddied by the fact that, in his report Wilson ignored recent meetings between representatives of Nigeria and Wissam al-Zahawie, an Iraqi diplomat who had actually brokered yellowcake deals between the two countries in the early 1980s. To add further confusion, forged papers emerged to "prove" latter day Iraq-Nigeria yellowcake deals, although these were easily debunked, throwing off any further investigation.

Did the CIA leak Plame's identity?

All of this skullduggery had conspiracy theorists seeing a clear CIA footprint. One theory was that Wilson's CIA wife had set him off on a mission designed to undercut the administration's foreign policy initiative (that is, the Iraq War), and the administration fought back with leaks about Plame's identity. This leak was in clear violation of the Intelligence Agent Identity Protection Act, which safeguards the identities of covert operatives. A special prosecutor was dispatched to locate and prosecute whoever had leaked the information.

In order to understand the issues of the Plame affair, the theorists turned to the history of this important piece of legislation, under which a number of successful prosecutions had previously been made. In 1969, for example, agent Victor Marchetti quit the CIA after becoming disillusioned in his job as a specialist in Soviet and Cuban affairs. He was expected to produce a tell-all book, and eventually co-authored *The CIA and the Cult of Intelligence* with John Marks. The book was so famously censored by the agency that it led to the congressional investigations of the intelligence services in the mid 1970s. During that period, the CIA also lost the highest ranking officer ever to resign, a man named John Stockwell. Stockwell's book, *In Search of Enemies*, met a successful CIA lawsuit that even today prevents him from making any money from it. In 1968, a third agent named Phillip Agee sued Barbara Bush, George W. Bush's mother, for suggesting that Agee had outed the CIA station chief in Greece, who was subsequently assassinated. Mrs. Bush had to retreat from the claim. However, in response to her suspicions Congress passed the Intelligence Identities Protection Act in order to make any such outing illegal in the future.

"It now had potential to strike at the foundation of George W. Bush's political architecture."

Changing image of the CIA

The image of the secret agent had changed in the US over the years. Though secret agents had once been seen as superheroic defenders of the West, perception of the agency during the Cold War went from one of beneficence to malevolence. The full details of CIA brainwashing programs like MKULTRA became apparent though congressional hearings in the 1970s, as did the CIA's secret assassination programs and its support for some of the world's worst dictatorships. It had become almost fashionable to "out" members of the evil agency. After 9/11, the Agency's image was damaged still further when theories began to circulate that the CIA had failed to protect the American people from the worst assault they had ever endured.

While many leftist critics stood firmly against the literary censorship of Marchetti, Stockwell, and Agee, support for the outing of Plame was very scant. The Intelligence Identities Protection Act now had potential to strike at the foundation of George W. Bush's political architecture. Karl Rove had, after all, directed two campaigns that brought Bush to presidential power and kept him there, and now he might have been charged with a criminal action (he never was). Political point-scoring rapidly replaced concerns over the identity of the agent exposed.

Prosecution unlikely to occur

Richard Armitage has confessed that he exposed Plame's name to columnist Robert Novak. Conspiracy theorists know Armitage's name well as a participant in the attempted cover-up of the Iran-Contra conspiracy. Armitage's confession of violating the Identities Protection Act came after prosecutor Patrick Fitzgerald issued indictments against Rove, later dropped, and Libby, over related charges rather than the actual violation of the act. There is some speculation that Armitage may be taking the fall for a more senior involvement. However, whatever damage the Plame affair eventually may do to the Bush administration, Armitage is not likely ever to be prosecuted for it.

The biggest spy scandal of the Bush administration raised more issues than it was ever likely to resolve. On March 6, 2007, Scooter Libby was found guilty of all but one of the charges against him, including perjury, obstruction of justice, and lying to federal investigators. He has yet to be sentenced at the time of writing, and is planning an appeal and a requested re-trial.

POINTS TO PONDER: MANIPULATION OF PUBLIC AFFAIRS

- At its base the Plame affair gets down to fundamental issues about covert manipulation of public affairs. The journalist Judith Miller spent three months in jail in 2005 for refusing to reveal the source for her New York Times report about Plame working for the CIA.
- When Robert Novak finally revealed who had leaked Plame's name to him, he made quite clear his opinion that the leak was no accident.
- "First, Armitage did not, as he now indicates, merely pass on something he had heard and that he 'thought' might be so," said Novak. "Rather, he identified to me the CIA division where Mrs. Wilson worked, and said flatly that she recommended the mission to Niger by her husband."
- "Second, Armitage did not slip me this information as idle chitchat, as he now suggests. He made clear he considered it especially suited for my column."

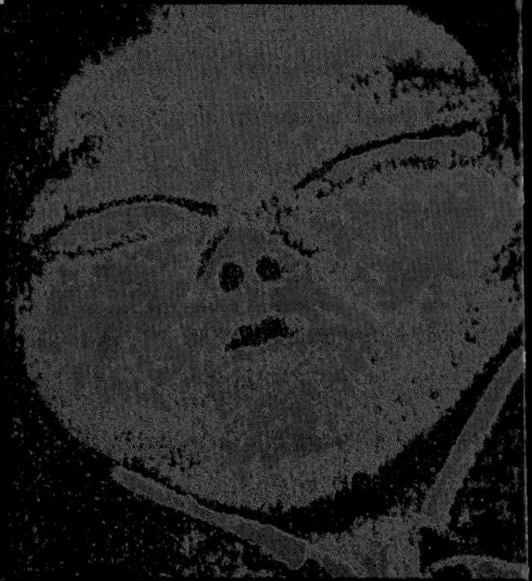

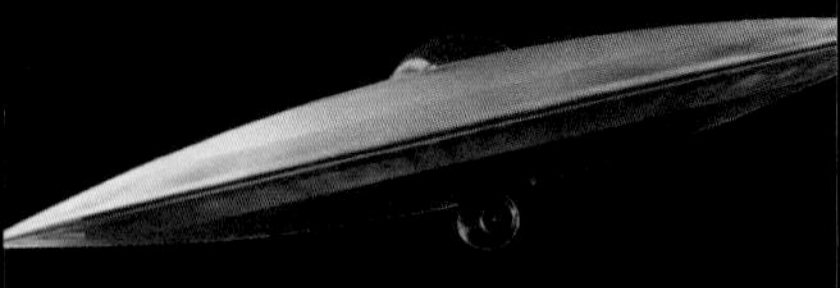

Science Faction

Who knows what tomorrow brings? The flying cars never arrived as promised in the first science fiction magazines. Instead, the future seems to hold more dystopian threats than utopian promises. Lee Harvey Oswald was a space-age spy; the space program itself may have had occult Nazi roots; and even the Internet was created by the Pentagon. Understanding conspiracy provides an illuminated view of the coming science-faction darkness.

Nazi UFOs

How advanced were the Nazi developments in aerospace weaponry during and after the World War II? Had their technology progressed so far as to enable them to have actually built, and flown, a flying saucer?

Right: The Germans are said to have continued their postwar space efforts from their South Pole colony of *Neu-Schwabenland*.

The German *Luftwaffe* excelled in aerospace weaponry. They created the V-2 rocket missile, responsible for the devastating blitz of Paris, London, and Antwerp during World War II. In 1939 they flew the first jet plane. They were also unsurpassed in the theoretical physics behind atomic bombs, creating the first nuclear fission reaction in Berlin in 1938. While these facts are now well documented, theorists also suggest that the Nazis worked on technological advances beyond rocket missiles, jets, and atomic power: that, in fact, they had produced and flown a flying saucer.

A witness account of an event in an airport hangar near Prague in February 1945 reported "a disk some 5 to 6 meters in diameter. Its body is relatively large at the center. Underneath, it has four tall, thin legs. Color: aluminum. Height: almost as tall as a man. Thickness: some 30 to 40 centimeters, with a rim of external rods, perhaps square orifices." The report of this sighting first appeared in the German flight magazine *Flugzeug* in February 1989. "Along with my friends," the reporter continued, "I saw the device emerge from the hangar. It was then that we heard the roar of the engines, we saw the external side of the disk begin to rotate, and the vehicle began moving slowly and in a straight line toward the southern end of the field. It then rose almost one meter into the air. After moving around some 300 meters at that altitude, it stopped again. Its landing was rather rough."

Opposite: Decoration telegram from the Third Reich, showing a *Luftwaffe* seaplane and a zeppelin.

Such a craft may have emerged from the work of Dr. Richard Miethe, a German scientist who, after World War II, joined the A. V. Roe Company in Canada and designed the disk-shaped, but largely

MEERWALD
LUFTHANSA
Deutsche Reichspost

earth-bound, Avrocar hovercraft (film footage of which is often used to depict UFOs.) Miethe and two other scientists, Klaus Habermohl and Rudolf Schreiver, reportedly worked on a secret Nazi UFO project known variously as *Haunebu* or *Flugdiskus*. According to some versions of the UFO story, however, the saucer at Prague reached an altitude in excess of 7.5 miles (12 kilometers) and a speed of 1200 mph (1930 kmph) in less than 3 minutes. That would be a fairly incredible feat, of course, and one certainly not reproducible by the Avrocar or even the craft in the *Flugzeug* report.

During the 1950s, a number of detailed technical sketches and blueprints began to circulate, along with stories about the work of Miethe, Habermohl, and Schreiver, that suggested technological designs even farther advanced than Nazi aerospace weapons. The stories included an Austrian forester, Viktor Schauberger, whose arcane research provided for the propulsion capacity of the craft, and which may have involved energized water or tonal harmonics. Schauberger frequently resurfaces in UFO literature as the true designer of the disk that was launched from Prague, having, as early as 1938, taken ideas regarding the turbine power of water and applied them to flying saucer design. The *Flugdiskus* team developed the earliest scale-model versions of the craft in 1942. Shortly afterward, Nazi command conscripted Schauberger to a UFO development project at the Mauthausen concentration camp. After the War, Schauberger continued his research work on experimental energy under American auspices and died in Chicago in 1958. Schauberger has been the subject of several biographies and interest in his ideas about the energetic properties of water remains within the alternative energy research community.

“In the mid-1970s Ernst Zundel, a former Canadian, published a book about the German flying saucers . . . and included the proposition that Nazi saucers still flew out of a base in the Antarctic.”

Critics maintain that many of the stories of German UFOs stem from modern-day Nazi sympathizers trying to add an exotic appeal to the ideology of fascism. In the mid-1970s Ernst Zundel, a former Canadian, published a book about the German flying saucers that referred to Viktor Schauberger and the flying disk of Prague, and included the proposition that Nazi saucers still flew out of a base in the Antarctic. In 1985, Zundel was convicted in a Canadian court for “publishing false news” and claiming that the Holocaust against the Jews had not happened. The Supreme Court of Canada struck down the law against “publishing false news,” however, after Zundel appealed his conviction in 1992.

Left: Conspiracy theorists suggest Nazi activity in the Antarctic, from bases for flying saucers to underground cities.

Other conspiracy researchers maintain more exotic theories about Nazi UFO propulsion. They trace the origins of Nazism to an occult lodge in 1920s Germany known as the Thule Society, which indulged in black magic to summon other-worldly spirits. The idea that occult forces could power flying saucers re-emerged among 1950s UFO contactees in America, such as George Adamski and George Hunt Williamson, who have been charged by various scholars with having neo-fascist sympathies and of being members of the CIA.

In the late 1940s, incidentally, the United States began to bring captured German rocket scientists into what became the first undisputed program to put a man on a celestial sphere other than the Earth. Former Nazis such as Werner Von Braun and Walter Dornberger helped create America's Apollo space program, which landed a man on the moon on July 20, 1969. Von Braun recounts, in his memoirs, an argument with JFK about what propulsion system should be used for the moon lander. As a rocket scientist, Von Braun says, he argued for rockets; what JFK had in mind, and whether it connected to occult Nazi UFO technology, is lost to history.

PEOPLE IN PURSUIT:

Vladimir Terziski

Vladimir Terziski was born in Sofia, Bulgaria. He went to America in 1985 as a political refugee, with degrees in physics and engineering from Tokai University in Japan. In Los Angeles, he opened the American Academy of Dissident Scientists and taught UFOlogy at a community center in Santa Monica, California.

Terziski believed that the Nazis landed on the Moon as early as 1942, utilizing their large exo-atmospheric rocket saucers of the Miethe and Schreiver design. "The Miethe rocket craft was built in diameters of 15 to 20 meters and the Schreiver water turbine-powered craft was designed as an interplanetary exploration vehicle. It had a diameter of 60 meters, had 10 stories of crew compartments, and stood 45 meters high." He concludes that from their first day on the Moon, the Nazis started tunneling under the surface, and that by the end of the War they had created a small research base. According to Terziski, the Nazis used the free energy drive of the *Haunebu 1* and *2* to haul people, materials, and the first robots to the construction site on the Moon. After the end of the War, in May 1945, the Germans continued their space effort from their South Pole colony of *Neu-Schwabenland*. When the Russians and Americans secretly landed on the Moon in the early 1950s with their own saucers, they spent their first night as guests at the Nazi base.

Vladimir Terziski lays claim to a large number of stories concerning anti-gravity flying devices from various times and cultures. He maintains that his research efforts penetrate a veil of secrecy surrounding advanced technology. "As a rule, I do not discard any bizarre story when I hear it," he says. "I will simply post it in the big mental picture of such posted messages, until there is a second similar story, and so on."

Terziski has extensive documentary evidence for anti-gravity and other forms of UFO propulsion that he has gathered from academic and tabloid sources, tracing such ideas through ancient legends and modern UFO lore. He asserts that "anti-gravity is extremely easy to produce. Simple rotation decreases the weight of a spinning body, and if you spin the hell out of it, it will lift off and fly away." Terziski insists that the better-built flying saucers move from slow-spinning heavy masses to "relativistic" spinning of high-frequency energy fields. With this in mind, his presentation retraces the origins of Nazi UFOs with documentary photographs, engineering drawings, and sketches of over 50 saucer models, including prototypes with gasoline pistons, propellers, and rotary engines. The material includes designs for hybrid helicopter rotor anti-gravity lift, gyroscoped and powered by outboard and inboard turbo, pulse, and ramjets. "My firm belief is that a rocket-spun, 18- to 45-meter diameter craft was capable of going to the Moon on a truckload of kerosene and a truckload of liquid oxygen, due to the magical keys to the saucer kingdom: the total negation of both gravitational and inertial masses when the anti-gravity drive starts spinning."

This was the knowledge the Nazis had, according to Terziski. "I was arrested and handcuffed by police in Pasadena, California, for showing four panels with the first and very detailed close-up photos in this country of low-flying Nazi saucer-shaped craft over testing grounds in Germany," he claims. "This happened after a lecture by Apollo 17 astronaut and ex-senator Harrison Schmidt in the Central Beckman Auditorium at the California Institute of Technology, the citadel of the party line in U.S. science. The lecture was on the planned twenty-first-century NASA flights to colonize Mars with inefficient and gas-guzzling rocket technology of today."

Terziski insists that such continued censorship of advanced space-flight propulsion is not unusual. "This is the very mode of operation of the terrestrial secret power elite, the evilarchy that rules the planet from behind the scenes. They usurp, hoard, and lock behind triple-vault doors the most advanced technologies that appear on the planet until they make sure that all the

Right: A disk-shaped craft built by Avro Aircraft Ltd. of Canada in 1960. It was abandoned in 1965 as it could not rise more than a few feet with stability.

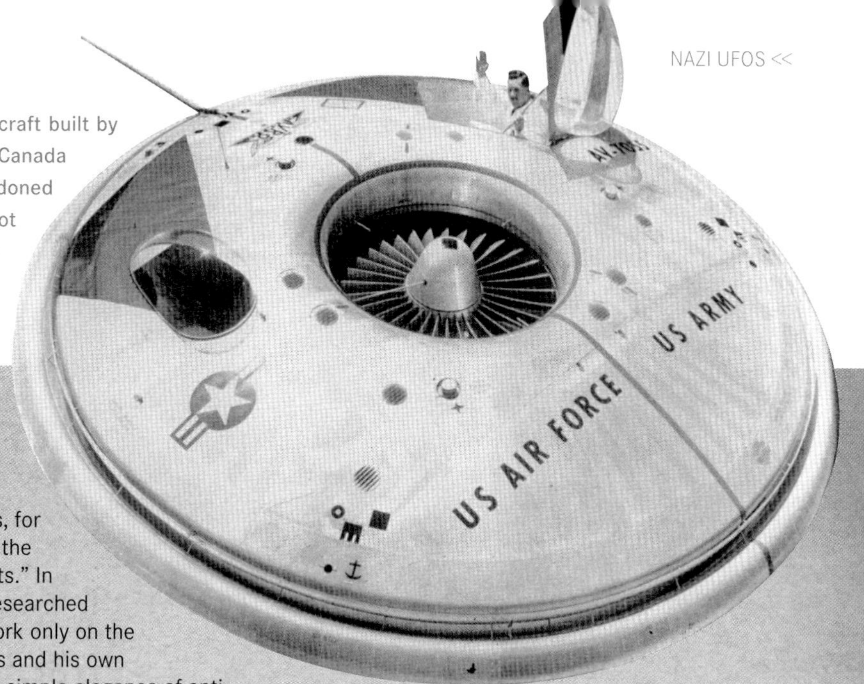

patents are in their possession and that the new technology will not undermine existing technologies, for which they also own the key patents and rights." In this belief, Terziski researched blindly, basing his work only on the lore of the Nazi UFOs and his own understanding of the simple elegance of anti-gravity propulsion potentials, until "private channels in Germany" sent what he regarded as credible documentary evidence.

These "channels" included the Thule Society, or *Thule Gesellschaft*, the occult secret society that boasted the most advanced free-energy saucers, powered by Viktor Schauberger's water turbines and the "tachyon magneto-gravitic drives" created by scientist Hans Kohler. Their documentation, according to Terziski, included dozens of photographs of low-level flights over testing grounds 10 meters in diameter, "Vril" series interceptor-fighters, 25-meter tank killers christened *Haunebu 1* and *2* types, and the 74-meter *Haunebu 3* dreadnought for anti-shipping warfare. Drawings of a *Haunebu 4* interplanetary craft 90 meters in diameter and a 100-meter-long cigar-shaped mothership dating from 1943 also appeared in the materials from *Thule Gesellschaft*.

Terziski became convinced that the flying saucers in World War II had no moving parts yet could fly to the Moon in under an hour, and that this was the least of their secrets. "It is much more important that they managed to do that without using a single drop of traditional fuel for the purpose," he explains. "The so-called free energy drives they were using were not *perpetuum mobile* drives that were producing energy out of nothing. They were converters of the practically inexhaustible gravitational energy of the Earth, Moon, or other planetary bodies that these craft were flying by, into the electro-magnetic energy necessary to propel the craft in space."

Thule Gesellschaft explained that the converter was coupled with a Van de Graaf band generator and a Marconi ball vortex dynamo in an electromagnetic-gravitic or tachyon drive, dubbed the Thule tachyonator. These were mass-produced on an assembly line at the AEG and Siemens plants in Germany from 1942 to 1945. The Nazis also used these converters to propel giant, 5000-ton transport submarines and to produce energy in underground bases around the world.

From *Thule Gesellschaft*, Terziski also learned that the Nazis began exploration of the South Pole with huge carrier ships in 1937. They proclaimed the landmass there, as large as the entire European continent, *Neu-Schwabenland*. In 1942 the *Kriegsmarine* began a massive evacuation of people and materials to the secret underground base planned as the last bastion of the Third Reich. Several hundred thousand concentration camp laborers, scientists, and Hitler Youth populated extensive German colonies at the South Pole to continue creating a society of *Übermensch*. According to Terziski, "The rumors are that there is a vast underground city nowadays under the South Pole with a population of two million, called–you guessed it–New Berlin. The major preoccupations of its inhabitants are human genetic engineering and space travel. Admiral Byrd is rumored to have secretly met with leaders of the German Antarctic colony in 1947, after his inglorious defeat, and to have concluded a condominium agreement with them."

Roswell

Is the town of Roswell in New Mexico synonymous with the United States government's ultimate cover-up of its involvement with extraterrestrial aliens?

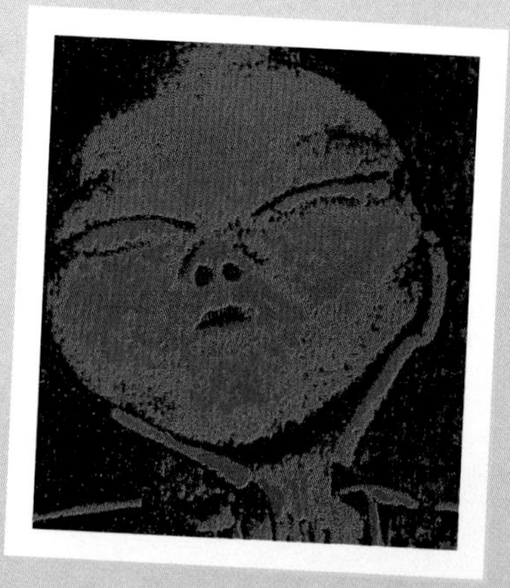

Right: A "genuine" photo of a Roswell alien that eventually turned out to be a photostat of an anonymous photograph of an alien plastic model.

"RAAF Captures Flying Saucer on Ranch in Roswell Region." The headline in the *Roswell Daily Record* of July 8, 1947, trumpeted not only the most renowned UFO incident in history but also the start of six decades of conjecture about what actually happened the previous night in that southeastern New Mexico town.

The details in the newspaper story were slight: Roswell Army Air Field had announced the recovery of a crashed "flying disk;" however, the intelligence office offered no further details on what this disk looked like or where it might have come from.

The *Roswell Daily Record* credited Dan Wilmot, "one of the most respected and reliable citizens in town," and his wife as the sole witnesses in Roswell to have seen such a disk some days before: "It looked oval in shape like two inverted saucers, faced mouth to mouth, or like two old-type washbowls placed together in the same fashion. The entire body glowed as though light were showing through from inside, though not like it would be if a light were merely underneath."

There was another witness to the crashed debris, however: a rancher named William "Mac" Brazel, who discovered it strewn across his farm and reported it to the Chaves County sheriff. It was then that matters took on a strange tone. The sheriff locked Brazel up for several days in order to ascertain what Brazel knew, but apparently also to encourage him to accept an official explanation that the debris had fallen from a weather balloon. Brazel had retrieved two such weather balloons in the past, but what he found this time "did not in any way resemble either of these." But it seems the sheriff made an impression upon Brazel because, on release, Brazel told the *Roswell Daily Record*: "I am sure that what I found was not any weather observation balloon. But if I find anything else, they are going to have a hard time getting me to say anything about it."

Major Jesse Marcel, the commanding intelligence officer of the 509th Bomb Group headquartered at the Roswell Army Base, recovered the debris from Brazel's ranch. The debris was then sent to Fort Worth, Texas, and on to Ohio's Wright-Patterson Air Force Base.

U.S. Air Force PR officer William Haut issued a press release, saying, "We have been fortunate enough to gain possession of a disk through the cooperation of one of the local ranchers," and the ABC wire service released a similar statement referring to the debris as a "flying saucer." ABC, however, denied the existence of witnesses to the crash, directly contradicting the *Roswell Daily Record*.

Conspiracy theories were further inflamed by some claims that witnesses had seen insectoid alien bodies with large, almond-shaped heads recovered from the saucer crash, being autopsied at the base and placed in child-sized coffins obtained from Roswell's Ballard Funeral Home. Indeed, in 1995, a grainy black-and-white film of an alien autopsy purportedly taken in 1947 at the Roswell Army Air Force Base was widely circulated, causing Dr. Chris Stinger of the Natural History Museum in London to remark, "If it's a fake, it's a brilliant one!"

"witnesses had seen insectoid alien bodies with large, almond-shaped heads recovered from the saucer crash, being autopsied at the base."

The main conspiracy stories surrounding Roswell relate that an alien ship crashed, and that the government recovered it and then back-engineered its technology at the Area 51 site in the New Mexico desert. Proponents of the theory point out the technological advances following the crash date: in the year 1947, mankind saw the development of holography, microwave ovens, the first practical nuclear reactors, nuclear submarines, transistors, and the breaking of the sound barrier. The following year saw Mount Palomar's 200-inch telescope become operable, as well as magnetic tape, magnetic drum data storage, Velcro, and cable TV. Vannevar Bush, a scientific adviser to President Eisenhower, was reportedly involved in the Roswell retrieval, and at the time wrote a remarkably prescient essay eerily describing today's personal computers.

The recovered debris comprised foil-like metal; an unusually light, balsa wood-like substance; and strange hieroglyphs—the materials were similar to those used in the construction of weather balloons. Indeed, General Roger Ramey, to whom Marcel had reported, was photographed with the remnants of such a balloon to accompany the newspaper report on the Roswell story. Students of the incident try to enlarge the telegram in Ramey's hand in that photograph, however, claiming that the message contains confirmation of an alien recovery.

The weather balloon theory was eventually to give way to the Fugo balloon theory, popularized by the writer John Keel. Keel claimed that at the end of World War II, the Japanese launched 9000 balloon bombs—the Fin-Go or Fugo balloons—and that it was one of these Fugo balloons that was recovered at Roswell. While the Japanese had deactivated the project in March 1945, a woman and five children were killed by an extant balloon two months later, in Lakeview, Oregon. A Fugo payload was found as recently as January 1955 in Alaska. But most of the Fugo balloon bombs failed to cross the ocean from Japan, and now there are few observers who accept the possibility that one could have stayed aloft for two years before crashing in New Mexico.

Then came the Project Mogul theory to explain the incident at Roswell. In September 1994 the U.S. Air Force issued a report admitting that its previous assessment of the debris as a weather

POINTS TO PONDER: ROSWELL, POINT AND COUNTERPOINT

- Research by UFOlogists has uncovered numerous witness statements that contradict the party line.
- Ranchers and Air Force personnel who had seen the wreckage insisted it was made of metals unknown to science.
- A woman who had worked for the military in the region spoke of bodies removed from the wreckage.
- A nurse at the Roswell base hospital gave details of the bodies, which were obviously not human. Several years later, in 1995, a film of an autopsy on the alien corpses surfaced.
- The government, of course, has a different story to tell. Officials say the "unearthly metals" were simply reflective material from one of the top-secret Project Mogul monitoring balloons, which were used to spy on Soviet nuclear tests.
- Government representatives say tales of recovered bodies are garbled memories from 1950s balloon tests involving crash-test dummies, or possibly from a fuel-plane wreckage where the corpses of the crew were badly burned.
- The nurse at the Roswell base hospital who is said to have passed on vital secret information never existed.
- The alien autopsy film, it has been generally accepted, is an imposture: the "alien" is an almost-exact replica of a model used in a film about Roswell. Meanwhile, the procedures caught on tape bear no resemblance to a real autopsy.

Left: General Roger M. Ramey (left), commander of Eighth Air Force, with the remains of the flying disk at his headquarters at Fort Worth, Texas, on July 8, 1947.

balloon was in error. Instead, they claimed, the debris had come from Project Mogul, a classified project in operation to acoustically monitor Soviet nuclear detonations at high altitudes. Scientists had lost track of one of their monitoring balloons 17 miles from Brazel's field.

The U.S. government adopted the Project Mogul explanation as its official line on Roswell after New Mexico Congressman Steven Schiff had the Government Accounting Office (GAO) initiate an audit of all records pertaining to the Roswell crash incident in 1994. Schiff belonged to the House Government Operations committee that oversees the GAO. He brought up the topic of Roswell at a routine meeting because of UFO stories he was regularly told by his constituents. He complained that the Department of Defense had been unresponsive to his inquiries and had tried to shunt him off to the National Archives. GAO controller General Charles Bowsher took an unusual initiative to pursue Schiff's interests, which ended with the detailed Project Mogul thesis. Schiff himself died aged 51 from skin cancer on March 25, 1998.

Author Nick Redfern presents a different theory in his book, *Body Snatchers in the Desert*. He concludes that the crash-site discovery of a prototype aircraft would have exposed the highly confidential U.S. government-sanctioned program to conduct medical experiments on deformed, handicapped, disfigured, and diseased Japanese prisoners of war, exploited as "expendable" by their captors. Redfern's account incorporates many new elements: the human experimentation work of Japan's notorious Unit 731 of World War II; advanced balloon designs of Japan's wartime scientific elite; controversial high-altitude exposure experiments at the White Sands Missile Range in New Mexico; and officially declassified documents on radiation experiments undertaken in the summer of

Philip Corso

CONSPIRACY LINKS:

"It was the 1950s, for God's sake," exclaimed Bill Birnes, Colonel Philip Corso's co-author and publisher. "Everybody was in a conspiracy! Walt Disney was in a conspiracy! There were so many, you didn't know who was conspiring for what!" Birnes's outburst, at the International UFO Congress in Laughlin, Nevada, came in response to a question about Philip Corso's connection to the Knights of Malta in Shickshinny, a town in eastern Pennsylvania. Birnes was standing in for the aging and ailing Corso at the Nevada event that day. Corso died shortly afterward.

Birnes had helped Corso write his 1997 book, *The Day After Roswell*, in which Corso, a retired U.S. colonel, claimed that many technological advances–integrated circuits, Kevlar, and silicon chips–came from back-engineered alien craft found at the New Mexico flying-saucer crash site. Corso's claims that he helped parcel out this technology as the lieutenant-colonel in charge of the Foreign Technology Desk in Army Research and Development at the Pentagon provided the basis for the book.

Corso's connections to the Shickshinny Knights had originally surfaced in a book by Dick Russell on the Kennedy assassination, *The Man Who Knew Too Much* (1992). Although *The Day After Roswell* was hailed as a great breakthrough for Roswell enthusiasts, it was considered by conspiracy researchers to have obfuscated rather than illuminated Corso's shadowy past. To those interested in military intelligence, other questions loomed larger than the Roswell aliens–questions, for example, about Corso's right-wing paramilitary

connections and his involvement in the plot to murder John F. Kennedy.

The Shickshinny Knights–formerly known as the Sovereign Order of St. John of Jerusalem and affiliated by coincidence of names to the Knights of Malta, a military order based in Italy–felt that the CIA was not pursuing the fight against Communism with sufficient vigor. They regarded the CIA as being soft in Central America. Their propaganda included promoting the stories of Michael Goliniewsky, a Polish intelligence officer who claimed to be Prince Alexi, heir to the Russian Tsar. Goliniewsky had defected to the West on the strength of what he revealed about KGB infiltration of Western intelligence. In his book, Russell argued that Corso and the Shickshinny Knights also worked to spread rumors that Lee Harvey Oswald belonged to a Communist ring within the CIA. Another noted JFK scholar,

1947 on people with *progeria*, a condition that results in a dwarf-like body; a large, bald head; and, occasionally, six fingers.

Roswell has an important connection to the history of aerospace engineering. Robert Goddard, the father of modern rocketry, did much of his later work there. The 509th Bomb Wing Composite Group stationed there played an instrumental role in the atomic bombings of Hiroshima and Nagasaki. In fact, some believe that nuclear testing in New Mexico first attracted aliens to Earth.

The town reinvented itself after the close of its Air Force base and today benefits from the tourist industry that has developed around alien themes and government conspiracy stories. Downtown Roswell boasts a Museum of UFO Studies and civic leaders annually hold a festival to celebrate the mystery of the crash.

Peter Dale Scott, asserted that the Shickshinny Knights planted information that connected Oswald to the Soviet Union and Jack Ruby to Fidel Castro's Cuba. Both writers agree that Corso's Shickshinny brotherhood contributed greatly to deflecting attention away from the real conspirators.

Chief among Corso's fellow Knights stood two prominent spies: Charles Willoughby, the former chief intelligence officer to General Douglas MacArthur; and William Gale, who later headed the Minutemen, the rightist militia group investigated by the Warren Commission. Strangely enough, Corso was appointed to be an investigator for the Commission in 1964.

After World War II, Corso helped repatriate the former Nazi spy network of Reinhard Gehlen into U.S. intelligence as part of Operation Paperclip. Prior to his work with the Warren Commission, Corso served as an assistant to C. D. Jackson, the official who co-wrote Eisenhower's "Atoms For Peace" speech. The scientist Wilhelm Reich claimed that the speech had been based on his ideas concerning the extraterrestrial threat. When Corso left military intelligence in 1963, he went to work as an assistant to the segregationist Senator Strom Thurmond, who wrote, but later repudiated, an introduction to the first edition of *The Day After Roswell*.

At that UFO conference in Nevada, Bill Birnes tried to respond to the suspicions of conspiracy, however nebulous, coloring his friend Corso's life: "Let's speak specifically to this issue of who knew what when. The issue that confronted Corso in 1963 was that he had known in advance of the [JFK] assassination and that the CIA had an operative in the Soviet Union called Lee Harvey Oswald. Corso knew–knew, not speculated–*knew* that the Soviet Union was creating what he called 'playbacks' out of U.S. service personnel in Korea, to come back and occupy new identities and perform acts of espionage against the United States. That's as far as I'm going to go about that. The man who knew too much? We know more."

Corso's military career concluded after 21 years with 19 ribbons, medals, and decorations for meritorious service. After his stint with Strom Thurmond and another senator, James Eastland, he retired as a contracts consultant and administrator. He served as a consultant to Congress and to the media, specializing in U-2 spy flights and prisoners of war during the Korean conflict. The book he produced at the end of his life appeared to be a tell-all about the most renowned case in the annals of UFOlogy, but now it is left to future biographers to fill in the more compelling issues of his life's story.

Eisenhower and the aliens

Did President Eisenhower meet with an alien race? Was he flown to Wright-Patterson Air Base on February 20, 1954, in order to view the remains of the Roswell flying saucer?

Right: Portrait of Eisenhower as Chief of Staff.

On February 20, 1954, it has been suggested, President Dwight D. Eisenhower was flown to Wright-Patterson Air Force Base in Ohio to view the debris of the alien craft that allegedly crashed at Roswell, New Mexico (see page 122). Conspiracy theorists believe that the president met with Nordic-looking creatures and began intergalactic peace talks with several alien races. Although the legend of the Roswell UFO crash persists, there is little actual proof. However, what evidential trail does exist provides some provocatively concrete detail. Archival documentation and historical sources come together remarkably to corroborate the involvement of Eisenhower with UFOs.

The president, who had just returned from a vacation in Georgia, was reported missing on the night of February 20 while enjoying a further vacation in Palm Springs. The official explanation for his disappearance was that he had lost a tooth cap while eating and had to make a late-night visit to a local dentist. There is scanty evidence of this. The widow of the dentist had only vague memories of the event, which by any measure, one imagines, would have made a lasting impression on her, and no record of the dental work appears in Eisenhower's medical record from his time as president. Was he in fact flown to Wright-Patterson Air Force Base that night to view the flying saucer wreckage recovered from the crash site at Roswell?

> "No record of the dental work appears in Eisenhower's medical record from his time as President."

Enter Wilhelm Reich

Wilhelm Reich's story begins in Vienna in the 1920s. With the ascendancy of the Nazis in Germany, Reich fled first to Norway and then on to America, moving away from his expertise in psychoanalysis and Marxism to focus on equally controversial ideas in biophysics. Reich had discovered what he termed "orgone," a biological energy found in living organisms and in the atmosphere. He reasoned that this energy could be used to combat UFOs, and there is documentary evidence to suggest that he met with Eisenhower around the time the president is said to have met with the aliens at Wright-Patterson Air Force Base.

Reich traveled through Roswell, New Mexico, on his way to Tucson, Arizona, carrying his orgone equipment in order to study its capacity to both alleviate desert conditions and do battle with UFOs. He recorded these experiences in his book, *Contact With Space*, now an underground classic. Although his immediate destination was Ruidoso Downs, New Mexico, there seems little doubt that Reich had aliens on his mind as he passed through Roswell.

Above: One of Wilhelm Reich's weather-influencing devices that also affect UFOs, and perhaps destroy them, 1954.

He wrote, "Although it was very hot as we neared Roswell, New Mexico, no OR [orgone] was visible on the road, which should have been shimmering with 'heatwaves.' Instead, DOR [deadly orgone radiation, which Reich believed came from the exhaust of UFOs] was seen in the sky to the west against the purplish, black, barren mountains, and as a grayish layer over the horizon. The caking of formerly good soil was progressively characteristic and eventually caked soil prevailed over any vegetation, which consisted of scattered low brushes, while grass disappeared."

Reich concluded, "After the desert valley it was a relief to spend a night in Ruidoso in the Sierra Blanca Mountains (near 7000 feet). Here a strong, reactive secondary vegetation had sprung up, again more marked on the western slope . . ."

Reich's concern about the environmental impact of UFOs stemmed from experiences he had had in Rangeley, Maine. It was there, in 1951, that he had first discovered DOR, the noxious reaction of the natural energy with nuclear material, which he called "deadly orgone." He put a milligram of radium into one of his orgone boxes (an invention he had created to accumulate and harness orgone.) It resulted in highly polluted air around the facility, with a seriously deleterious effect on fauna and animals. DOR clouds formed and a strange black substance fell on the area. Strange, red pulsating lights appeared in the sky. In response to this, Reich later invented the cloudbuster gun, which intensified and redirected the healthy orgone, causing the pulsating lights to twinkle out, and diminishing the DOR effect on the environment.

Unreliable evidence

Skeptics of the Roswell story often claim that interest in the event dropped off immediately after its initial media attention. However, interest was revived in the late 1980s by UFO researchers. Reich's visit to Roswell, which makes clear references to aliens, and the remarkably strong archival documentation from several disparate sources, show that there may be a connection between Reich and Dwight Eisenhower.

First, there is the Cutler-Twining memo. The National Archives in Washington, DC, holds the onion-skinned carbon of a memo calling for the postponement of a Special Studies Section of the group MJ-12. UFOlogists recognize MJ-12 as the group allegedly started by Harry Truman in response to the Roswell crash, to deal secretly with the alien presence. But skeptics claim that the document—dated July 14, 1954, five months after Eisenhower's supposed meeting with the aliens—is fake and was smuggled into the archives. Whether unwilling or unable to verify the authenticity of this document (by paper-lot and typewriter style dating), the National Archives has nevertheless retained it for a half-century.

The author of the memo, Robert Cutler, served in the CIA under Eisenhower in its Division of Psychological Operations. Cutler wrote Eisenhower's famous "Atoms for Peace" speech, which took as its title a phrase used by Wilhelm Reich to describe his orgone work. The recipient of the memo, Nathan Twining, is well-known to students of UFOlogy as the general to whom Air Force investigators reported UFO sightings and retrievals. One such retrieval, involving flying saucers in the Maury Island area in the Pacific northwest, also involved the kind of black substance that Reich had described at his lab in Maine.

The second curious document in the research was recovered only recently by author Jim Martin, as part of his comprehensive look at Wilhelm Reich's life in the 1950s, entitled *Wilhelm Reich and the Cold War*. Martin discovered what has become known as the Moise-Douglas memo in the archives of Lew Douglas, a member of Eisenhower's "kitchen cabinet" who was assigned to a presidential committee on weather control. In *Contact With Space*, Reich claimed that he had corresponded with Douglas; Martin asserted that this discovered memo was the proof. The memo was sent by Douglas and describes several recent failed attempts by Reich's assistant, William Moise, to make contact. Although the memo itself is not dated, a handwritten note at the bottom indicates a change of heart by Douglas, who ultimately did telegraph Moise on July 27, 1954.

This timeline is perhaps the best indication in the records that MJ-12 existed and, by inference, that Eisenhower met with aliens. Douglas's about-face with regard to Reich, coming at any point in July 1954, indicates that he had been briefed at the MJ-12 meeting described in the Cutler-Twining memo. The object of the Special Studies Project was Reich's counterattack on UFOs, and Douglas was directed to take a greater interest in it. In the end, Douglas wound up bankrolling, in part, some of Reich's environmental work in Tucson.

Above: Portrait of Wilhelm Reich (1897-1957) surrounded by relevant arcane symbols. Reich believed he had identified etheric energy, which he named orgone.

Finally, there is Reich's own meeting with Eisenhower. One witness claimed that during a hunting and fishing trip to Rangeley, Maine, where Reich's laboratory was located, Eisenhower met with the inventor of the anti-UFO technology. The Eisenhower Library records a visit to Rangeley during that period, from June to July 1955. In the end, however, the witness's memory is as vague as that of the dentist's widow, who had but scant recollection of Eisenhower's visit the year before.

The trail evaporates after that, only to re-emerge just one more time. According to the biography of his second wife, the screen comedian Jackie Gleason caught a glimpse of alien bodies in 1973 at the behest of President Richard Nixon. Nixon had, of course, been Eisenhower's vice president. He took his friend Gleason to a secret facility in Palm Springs, from where Eisenhower is said to have disappeared that one night for his alleged visitation with aliens all those years before.

Does this amount to proof that such creatures exist and that Eisenhower met them? No absolute proof can be offered.

Reich was eventually prosecuted for his orgone devices, which were characterized as bogus cancer-cure machines. A technical violation of an injuction from the Food and Drug Administration led to Reich's imprisonment. Federal authorities destroyed much of his scientific equipment and had his books burned. Many believe that the prosecution resulted from powerful medical and pharmaceutical interests that had been threatened by Reich's work. Reich died in prison in 1957.

In his retirement speech in January, 1961, Eisenhower coined the phrase "military-industrial complex," and conjured up an image of Wilhelm Reich, his possible secret ally in the war against extraterrestrials. "Today," Eisenhower noted, "the solitary inventor, tinkering in his shop, has been overshadowed by task forces of scientists in laboratories and testing fields . . . A government contract becomes virtually a substitute for intellectual curiosity. The prospect of domination of the nation's scholars by Federal employment, project allocations, and the power of money is ever present . . ."

"There is no use in trying to prove something that is unknown to somebody who is ignorant of the unknown, or fearful of its threatening power."

Although the record suggests that Reich had interest and support from the Eisenhower administration in his battles against UFOs, he had never sought it. He believed in spaceships piloted by extraterrestrials and regarded contact with them as a logical event, not simple sightings of craft: he needed no stamp of approval from government authority to make this claim.

PEOPLE IN PURSUIT:

James DeMeo

Despite the great controversies surrounding the life and career of Wilhelm Reich–controversies that led to his arrest, the burning of his books, and an early death–a few scientists around the globe have continued to work with his ideas and their practical application. Chief among them is James DeMeo, PhD, who runs the Orgone Biophysical Research Laboratory (OBRL) in forested, rural Ashland, Oregon. Unique among scientific facilities in the United States, OBRL's Greensprings Center uses a passive solar-heating design and includes a large-aperture Newtonian Reflector telescope. It houses a number of orgone accumulators and cloudbusters in current research use.

In 1977, as part of his graduate research, DeMeo began a study of Reich's cloudbuster at the Geography-Meteorology Department of the University of Kansas (KU), validating the device for the first time by peer review within a mainstream academic institution. Like Reich, DeMeo went on to use the device in desert regions of the American southwest to induce rain, a process he repeated in the 1990s in cloudbuster expeditions to Namibia, Israel, and Eritrea, each one supported by the local governments. Not unlike Reich, DeMeo encountered resistance from the scientific establishment.

"From the moment my research data at KU provided support for Reich, everyone on my research committee started feeling immense heat to abandon the project from the National Science Foundation [NSF] and the National Academy of Sciences in Washington, DC," says DeMeo. "At one point, the NSF threatened to cut off all funding for every project in every department within the entire university, unless my little project researching the cloudbuster was terminated." The reaction put to an end any formal support for DeMeo's cloudbuster work at

"There is no proof," wrote Reich in *Contact With Space*. "There are no authorities whatever. No President, Academy, Court of Law, Congress, or Senate on this earth has the knowledge or power to decide what will be the knowledge of tomorrow. There is no use in trying to prove something that is unknown to somebody who is ignorant of the unknown, or fearful of its threatening power. Only the good old rules of learning will eventually bring about understanding of what has invaded our earthly existence."

Right: Wilhelm Reich's orgone box, called an "orgone accumulator," in which patients could sit.

the university. DeMeo had no regrets, however, since the snub drove him further into the more controversial aspects of Wilhelm Reich's legacy. "I quit universities in 1988, going independent with OBRL thereafter," he explains. He wrote a handbook on how to use orgone accumulators that was eventually translated into seven languages. Most importantly, he developed his research on the region he identified as Saharasia, discovering a global pattern in human behavior linking violence to harsh deserts.

In 1998, DeMeo published a book entitled *Saharasia*, which presented his decade-long study (a revised edition was published in 2006.) His human behavior maps, he argues, led to the discovery of the Saharasian "origins of violence" and the historical source of patriarchal authoritarian society. "It solved the riddle of what Reich called the origins of armoring. The research demonstrates that the origins of human violence reside in traumatic and sex-repressive social institutions during the historically unprecedented epoch of drought, desertification, famine, and mass migrations that gripped the Saharasian region of the Old World from circa 4000 BCE."

Today, DeMeo travels widely developing his thesis and accruing research verification. He also publishes the research journal *Pulse of the Planet*. At OBRL (www.orgonelab.org), in addition to carrying out work involving orgone devices, the center hosts regular seminars and educational events concerning current applications of Reich's scientific accomplishments in the context of DeMeo's later research.

Evolution

Did the Cold War inhibit the understanding and acceptance of the science of evolution, after the USSR's adoption and distortion of Lamarckian concepts, which were consequently rejected by the Western world?

Right: Charles Darwin (1809–1882).

Charles Darwin's theory of natural selection underpins our understanding of evolution, but debate in some scientific circles suggests that the case has not yet been definitively closed on this key evolutionary mechanism. Darwin's natural-selection model of random mutation may well still compete with Jean-Baptiste Lamarck's law of the inheritance of acquired characteristics, researchers suggest. But how were Lamarck's theories first pushed aside and discredited in the Western world?

Jean-Baptiste Lamarck (1744–1829) was a French naturalist and distinguished botanist who in 1801 began to publish his theories on evolution. He held that changes in the environment caused changes in the needs and behaviors of an organism, which in turn resulted in the organism adapting its structure to the new environment. These physiological changes, he postulated, were heritable; according to him, generations could learn—that is, encode in their genetic structure—the lessons imparted to previous generations. Although even Darwin himself later acknowledged Larmarck, in 1861, as a "justly celebrated naturalist" who carried out "eminent service" in the study of the organic and inorganic worlds, the Frenchman's evolutionary theories were never globally accepted, neither in his lifetime nor in later years.

Lamarck in the twentieth century and beyond

Arthur Koestler, in his book *The Case of the Midwife Toad*, documents how, when Darwinian evolution was already the accepted paradigm, Paul Kammerer, an Austrian biologist, set out to show that Lamarckism was the true key to the transformation of species. During

Left: Jean-Baptiste Lamarck (1744–1829), circa 1800. His theories on evolution were adopted by the USSR.

the 1920s, Kammerer carried out studies on the midwife toad to prove the Lamarckian law of inherited traits. This species of toad lacks the gripping characteristics possessed by other male toad species, by which they hold on to the females during mating in their watery environment. The midwife toad mates on dry land and so does not require nor has acquired such equipment. Kammerer put generations of midwife toads in water and claimed that, sure enough, they developed the secondary sexual characteristics.

Kammerer presented his findings to the scientific community, Koestler recounts, only to have them met with criticism and jealous reactions, primarily from a Cambridge geneticist named William Bateson. The resulting ridicule of Kammerer, and the sabotage of his experimental work by an assistant, led to the young biologist's suicide.

"If Kammerer's experiments were regarded as unrepeatable," noted Koestler, "the blame lies on those who tried to repeat them with inadequate methods," referring to Bateson. Mark Gillman also wrote about the incident in his aptly named book, *Envy As A Retarding Force in Science*.

Nevertheless, Kammerer became a hero of science in the Soviet Union. The USSR's chief scientific bureaucrat, T. D. Lysenko, vulgarized the law of inheritance of acquired characteristics by imposing it on Soviet agricultural practices, just as Stalin had vulgarized Marxist tenets during his reign. Lysenko named the agricultural technique "vernalization." His claim of great success in seed germination flew in the face of the facts, however, and consequently destroyed the Soviets' credibility with geneticists throughout the world. That the world was further deterred from exploring the principles of Lamarckian evolutionary theory was an unfortunate side effect.

Further resistance to Lamarck in the West came in the form of the Weismann barrier, named after August Weismann, a German professor of comparative anatomy and zoology. In the 1880s and '90s, Weismann cut off the tails of several generations of rats to demonstrate that no descendant rat was born without a tail. He further noted that the Jews had been effectively carrying out the same experiment for millennia by circumcizing their male children, who nonetheless continue to father sons born with foreskins.

PEOPLE IN PURSUIT:

Arthur Koestler

In his book *The Case of the Midwife Toad*, Arthur Koestler chronicled how the Lamarckian view of evolution became lost to science. He attributes this to a conspiracy to discredit the biologist Paul Kammerer.

The book did not mark Koestler's only foray into parapolitical subjects. Koestler took his keen intellectual hammer and tongs to many topics. For instance, his original sympathies for Communism were reversed after the show trials in Stalin's Soviet Union in the late 1930s, when former Bolsheviks confessed to false conspiracies. Koestler became a staunch anti-Communist, like his contemporary George Orwell, and denounced his Communist past in an essay for the book *The God That Failed*, and in his seminal political novel *Darkness at Noon*.

In Koestler's 1976 book, *The Thirteenth Tribe*, he presented his view on the origins of the Eastern European Ashkenazi Jews, arguing, in an attempt to assuage anti-Semitic sentiment, against a historic connection to the Jews of the Bible. Nevertheless, the argument has been used by conspiracy theorists to diminish Jewish claims on Israeli-occupied territories of the Middle East.

Other topics explored by Koestler include synchronicity, the civil rights of suicide, ESP, LSD, the parapolitics of astronomy, and the creative process itself. By the end of his long career, Arthur Koestler had become an important figure to conspiracy theorists.

Koestler remains one of the most articulate spokesmen concerning UFOs and the impulse behind the apparent need of authorities to deny and cover up an experience that many people have found to be quite real. In his history of astronomy, *The Sleepwalkers*, Koestler compares the situation to the one faced by Galileo in 1610 when he tried to show the moons of Jupiter to several clerics, using a telescope into which they refused to look. Although Galileo had the best instrument available at the time, it was still quite crude. "Thus it was not entirely unreasonable to suspect the blurred dots which appeared to the strained and watering eye pressed to the spectacle-sized lens, might be optical illusions," writes Koestler. "The whole controversy about optical illusions, haloes, reflections from luminous clouds, and about the unreliability of testimonies, inevitably reminds one of a similar controversy

Serious debate occured in Soviet journals on this topic, but the fact remained that since Western scientists could conceive of no Lamarckian mechanism, for most of the last century, no such mechanism existed. In *Heredity and Environment* (1915), Princeton University professor E. G. Conklin criticized Weismann's argument: "Even if we could conceive of no mechanism for [a] purpose, this does not preclude the existence of such a mechanism." Today, the question posed by the Weismann barrier is addressed primarily in terms of how Weismann's experiments side-stepped a fundamental Lamarckian principle: Weismann's tail-cutting had nothing to do with a genetic response adaptive to the rat's environment.

Ultimately, theories, too, evolve. In their 2001 book *Lamarck's Signature,* Australian biologists Edward J. Steele, Robyn A. Lindley, and Robert V. Blanden shed new light on the notion of random mutation that underlies current concepts of evolution. While not displacing the importance and predominance of natural selection, their research suggests that Larmarck's principles have particular application to structures within the body's immune system. Jean-Baptiste Lamarck may yet come to pose a significant intellectual challenge in contemporary debate on evolution.

three hundred years later: the flying saucers. Here, too, emotion and prejudice combined with technical difficulties against clear-cut conclusions. And here, too, it was not unreasonable for self-respecting scholars to refuse to look at the photographic "evidence" for fear of making fools of themselves. Similar considerations may be applied to the refusal of otherwise open-minded scholars to get involved..."

Right: Arthur Koestler (1905–1983), the Hungarian author of one of the last century's great political novels, *Darkness at Noon.*

Maury Island

Was there a genuine UFO sighting at Maury Island in 1947? Was witness Harold Dahl forced into silence and denial by a government organization in an attempt to conceal the incident? Or was the entire story simply a hoax?

Right: Cover of *Fate* magazine from 1954, featuring a story on a UFO sighting.

Opposite: An artist's impression of Captain Thomas Mantell, Junior, chasing a UFO in his P-51 Mustang fighter plane.

Along the shore of a bay around Maury Island, in Puget Sound in Washington state, on June 21, 1947, a man named Harold Dahl was working to salvage the timber that breaks free along the shipping routes of the lumber companies; salvagers get paid for capturing and returning the timber. As Dahl, his son, their dog, and two others worked from their vessel, *North Queen*, they encountered UFOs in the sky above them. At about 2 PM, Dahl spotted six disk-shaped flying craft. One in the middle wobbled and five others surrounded it, all at an elevation of about 2000 feet.

Dahl described the flying saucers as being 25 feet (7.6 m) in diameter. He said they looked like donuts, right down to the hole in the middle. They were flattened at the center, concave not convex, with five-foot-wide portholes on their sides. Dahl said they were gold and silver, and said they shone "like a Buick's dashboard." At the base of each of the flying donuts was one dark porthole that spun around.

Dahl pulled out his camera and took some photographs. The middle saucer wobbled and dropped down about 200 feet from the others. It dropped another 500 feet and stopped wobbling before one of the circling saucers broke formation, flew down, touched the other one, and became still itself. Dahl said it looked as if the second one was giving assistance to the one that had been wobbling.

Then the saucers started spewing out two different substances. The central saucer released a white substance, which Dahl described as a thin, white, "newspaper-like" metal that more or less floated down into the bay. A second substance was released that Dahl

83N
US AF

described as black and similar to lava rock. The chunks that fell into the bay were so hot they caused steam to rise. Some pieces flew down onto the shore and onto the boat's crew. Harold's son Charles was struck in the arm by some of the lava rock. Another piece hit and killed the dog, making it the first casualty of the modern UFO era—a distinction that is usually given to Thomas Mantell, a U.S. Air Force captain who crashed his F-51 in January 1948 in pursuit of a UFO whose description matched that of the Maury Island saucers.

What happened near Maury Island on that day in 1947 was just the beginning of the story. After the saucers departed, Dahl and his crew threw the dog's body into the water and collected samples of both the white and the black substances. They were anxious to get medical treatment for Charles Dahl. While the injury to his arm was slight, he would later face a bizarre set of circumstances, which would in part cause his father to claim that the UFO encounter was a hoax. Before that, however, Harold Dahl told his story to a man named Fred Crisman.

Crisman was a man with a long and complicated life story. He seems to have had a career that kept one foot in covert intelligence and another in the world of conmen, hustlers, and bums. Crisman is often described as the dominant partner in his relationship with Dahl, perhaps even putting Dahl up to carrying on a hoax. The record shows, however, that Crisman had no official authority over Dahl, which adds some veracity to the idea that both men told the truth without coercion.

Crisman's involvement with the Maury Island saucer story began two days after Dahl's encounter. As Dahl had expected, Crisman thought that he and the crew had been drunk when they saw the saucer incident. But since Dahl had samples of the lava rock and told him that more could be found along the shoreline, Crisman decided to take a look. He did indeed see a large amount of white and black material, but as he looked it over, a donut-shaped craft, just as Dahl had described, appeared in the sky above him. According to Crisman, it was a very brief encounter, but scary enough to send him running.

"It was a very brief encounter, but scary enough to send him running."

Amazing stories

So who was Fred Crisman? His earliest appearance in the media was in the form of an extensive quote in *Harper's* magazine in September 1946, in an article about the first postar world convention on science fiction, held the preceding March in New York.

Harper's quoting of Crisman led to his angry response, printed in the May 1947 issue of *Amazing Stories*, a science fiction pulp magazine. In the piece, Crisman complained that the original article in *Harper's* amounted to nothing more than armchair philosophizing about science fiction concepts that he considered to be real phenomena, and had nothing to do with flying saucers.

The idea of advanced aircraft had been around for a long time, of course. Science fiction has an established history in print, on the radio, and at the movies. The *Flash Gordon* serials of the 1930s, for instance, featured various rocket-type ships, and UFOs of all shapes and stripes have been around for centuries, but the imagery of the flying saucer as a recurring theme began in the late 1940s, just after the first wave of sightings.

Above: Cover of *Fate* magazine, featuring a story on the UFO seen by Ray Stanford at Padre Island, Texas, on November 6, 1954.

The publisher of *Amazing Stories* was Ray Palmer, who helped popularize and promote the idea of flying saucers in his many pulp magazines. In the 1990s, Steven Spielberg produced a television version of *Amazing Stories*, using the pulp magazine format.

Palmer more than doubled the circulation of his various magazines by introducing "true stories," told by Richard Shaver, about a mysterious race of beings known as the deros. The deros were an underground alien race that looked very much like the "little grays" commonly described by people who claim to have been abducted by outer space aliens. Shaver and Palmer insisted on the reality of the deros. Deros were alien creatures inhabiting caverns deep in the Earth's core, Shaver claimed, but all Earth men are also in part dero because they are affected by detrimental energy streams in the post-atomic world ("dero" contracts the words "detrimental" and "robot.") Shaver's stories reflected the discomfort that many science fiction fans felt in the fledgling nuclear age after the end of the War. The interest in these stories became so great that it not only increased the circulation of Ray Palmer's magazines, it also led many readers to write their own stories about encounters with the deros.

Fred Crisman was one such contributor. After his quote appeared in *Harper's*, Crisman wrote a letter to *Amazing Stories*, describing an encounter with the deros in Burma, during which he had been wounded in the arm by what sounded eerily like a laser—years before lasers were developed.

Kenneth Arnold's chevron sighting

The U.S. Air Force captain Thomas Mantell, and the Maury Island dog, might have been the first two UFO casualties, but 32 marines had crashed into a site at Mount Rainier in Washington state the previous December. In July 1947, three days after Dahl's and Crisman's encounters near Maury Island, Kenneth Arnold, a businessman and pilot, was investigating the disappearance of the marines' C-47 transport plane to discover what had happened to it and its occupants. The official cause of the crash was that the aircraft had veered off course but some investigators suggested that the marines had died as result of an encounter with a flying saucer, maybe even damaging one in the collision so that it required the repair maneuver over Maury Island. In any event, investigators had found only small pieces of wreckage of the C-47 and the tattered remains of one marine uniform. With the promise of a US$5000 reward, Arnold was flying a small plane over Mount Rainier to find the rest of the remains when he had his own UFO sighting.

"32 marines had died as result of an encounter with a flying saucer, maybe even damaging one in the collision."

Arnold's reported sighting of nine UFOs, eight of them semi-circular and one of them crescent-shaped, triggered an enormous wave of UFO sightings in the late 1940s. In the *East Oregonian* newspaper, 17 UFO sightings were reported in the month following Arnold's sighting. National newspapers were filled with many similar reports. More often than not the UFOs described matched the description of the Maury Island saucers rather than those described as chevrons by Arnold.

In some incidents, people actually recovered the saucers. One housewife discovered a 30-inch saucer in her yard and turned it over to the FBI. It was gold-plated on one side and silver on the other, the same as the Maury Island craft. Oddly enough, the size and shape of it matched a second, lesser-known sighting by Kenneth Arnold on July 29 of that year. Newspapers later declared that four young pranksters had built it using parts from an old phonograph, but that story emerged only after some strange actions by the authorities. The FBI agent in charge, Guy Banister, called in army intelligence officers who locked the saucer in a back room. They instructed local police not to say a word about it.

Banister had served as a special agent in charge (SAC) for the FBI in Idaho and Montana at the time of the Maury Island case in Washington. In the 1950s he testified before a legislative committee in Louisiana that in the decade before he had spent time working in counter-espionage. In his testimony, he described the saucer as a Japanese Fugo balloon bomb (which exposed the story of the four boys rearranging parts of a record player as a possible fabrication).

Below: Kenneth Arnold with a drawing of one of the UFOs he saw over Mount Rainier.

Above: A Japanese 30-foot (10-m) diameter Mulberry paper balloon bomb.

The Fugo balloon theory has been offered up as one of the many explanations for the UFO event at Roswell, New Mexico, the following month (see page 122). That theory has been almost totally debunked, since the Fugo balloons were launched from Japan in March 1945, and the possibility of them staying aloft for such a long period is remote. Incidentally, Banister's Louisiana testimony included acknowledgment that he was also a coordinator for a right-wing militia group called the Minutemen, the only such group questioned by the Warren Commission investigation into the JFK assassination.

Arnold investigates Dahl and Crisman

Ray Palmer of *Amazing Stories* read about Kenneth Arnold's chevron sighting in the newspaper and wrote to him asking for details. Arnold sent him a copy of the report he had made to the Air Force, and Palmer wrote back and offered him US$200 to investigate the Maury Island sightings. Knowing nothing of Palmer's previous connection to Crisman, Arnold took it on.

The investigation was curious from the start. Arriving at Tacoma's Linnard-Western Winthrop Hotel in order to conduct interviews with Dahl and Crisman, Arnold discovered that a room had already been reserved in his name by persons unknown.

Harold Dahl was reluctant to talk to Arnold but eventually agreed to take him to the storage site of the debris he had recovered from Maury Island. Fred Crisman showed up at the Winthrop the next day and went over his version of the Maury Island story with Arnold. He also told him of his flight missions over Burma during the War, although he mentioned nothing of the deros. Afterward, Arnold suggested that they go out to Maury Island, and it was then that Arnold decided to bring along Emil Smith. Smith was an airline captain who had publicly derided Arnold about his Mount Rainier experience but had then had a UFO encounter of his own. Arnold had met him through a military intelligence officer, Paul Weiland (who, incidentally, had been a judge at the Nuremburg trials.)

When Emil Smith met Crisman and Dahl, the two men recounted the Maury Island sightings again and agreed to meet at the island the next day with more samples of the lava rock. Crisman volunteered to drive Smith on a long trip to Seattle and back to recover his personal items.

Before Arnold and Smith turned in that night, they received a call from Ted Morello, a United Press International (UPI) reporter who, instead of asking for information, repeated back to the pair the conversations they had had with Dahl. It appeared the room at the Winthrop had been bugged.

> "They received a call from Ted Morello, a reporter who, instead of asking for information, repeated back to the pair the conversations they had had with Dahl. It appeared the room at the Winthrop had been bugged."

Arnold decided to call in the U.S. Air Force. Crisman was excited about the idea but Dahl refused to talk to anyone from military intelligence. Nevertheless, through Arnold's connection with Weiland, two Air Force investigators from the Fourth Air Force A-2 Intelligence unit, Captain William Lee Davidson and First Lieutenant Frank Mercer Brown, came to the Winthrop Hotel.

Arnold knew Davidson and Brown from the investigation into his Mount Rainier sighting. The two Air Force investigators had an ongoing assignment to collect as much information as possible on the 1947 summer wave of UFOs. They had been dispatched by General Carl "Ptooey" Spaatz, a commander who served in Italy during the War as a part of Project Ultra, a decryption project similar to the Magic decryption project in Japan. Spaatz had provided Davidson and Brown with a B-25 to collect this information, particularly on cases that involved saucer recoveries. They reported to the Air Technical Intelligence Command at Wright-Patterson Air Force Base in Ohio. According to an FBI memo from August 1947, Spaatz, Brown, and Davidson in turn all reported to General Nathan Twining.

When Arnold turned over many of the letters he had received from people following the reports of his sighting in the newspapers, Davidson and Brown expressed a particular interest in the letter received from Ray Palmer. Though Dahl repeated the story to the investigators with reluctance, Crisman readily offered details about the white debris collected and made it seem much like the material recovered in the Roswell crash.

The "Men in Black"

After Harold Dahl first began talking to people about the UFO sightings, he had an experience that was shared by other UFO witnesses: he received a visit from a "Man in Black." The man drove a black Buick and demonstrated, when he met with Dahl, that he had a detailed knowledge of Dahl's Maury Island experience. He told Dahl that if he let the Maury Island story out, bad things would start happening to his family. Shortly afterward, Dahl lost a large number of logs he had salvaged from the bay, severely damaging his business; his wife fell ill; and Charles, his son, disappeared and was eventually found busing tables and suffering total amnesia. Faced with these crises, Dahl elected to explain that the whole Maury Island incident had been a hoax.

"Dahl lost a large number of logs, severely damaging his business; his wife fell ill; Charles, his son, disappeared and was eventually found bussing tables and suffering total amnesia."

Other anomalies haunted the Maury Island investigation. When Arnold had first called Air Force Lieutenant Brown, Brown had refused to accept the call on the military line: he chose to call Arnold back on a pay phone. Moments later, the UPI reporter Morello called again, demonstrating that he knew all about the military investigators. There were discrepancies in material evidece as well: Brown and Davidson supposedly took from their investigation the recovered debris, in what has been described variously as a large trunk or a small Kelloggs Corn Flakes packet. Meanwhile, Arnold described the material as differing from what Dahl had brought to him at the hotel.

In a bizarre development, Davidson and Brown were killed when their B-25 crashed the next day. A counterintelligence team found no evidence of the Maury Island debris at the crash site. The team recommended that any similar incidents be handled by the Foreign Technologies Desk of the U.S. Army's Department of Research and Development. Kenneth Arnold and Emil Smith dropped their investigation after the deaths of Davidson and Brown.

Harold Dahl continued to live in Tacoma, near Maury Island, although his salvage work never recovered after the encounter with the "Man in Black." He died in 1980.

Some conspiracy researchers suggest that the material given to Davidson and Brown may have been, according to one document of questionable provenance, "celestial fragments containing metal from a nuclear reactor from a UFO. The fragments were turned over to CIA agent Clay Shaw and Crisman was ordered to the Alaskan ADC for assignment in Project IVI." Crisman returned to Alaska after the Maury Island incident and the military reactivated him for service in the Korean War. He died in Tacoma in 1975.

As for the investigators themselves, Smith retired to Florida, and Arnold went on to more fame as a result of his own UFO sighting. In fact, he became a national celebrity and gave lectures at UFO conferences across the United States. Although the Maury Island story appears in his book, *The Coming of the Saucers,* it does not comprise a major part of the story he tells.

POINTS TO PONDER: RELATED UFO HOAXES

- A researcher named Ron Halbritter suggests that the Maury Island saucers, Kenneth Arnold's chevrons, and whatever may have crashed at Roswell, were all the same craft. Crisman's description of the white metal certainly matches descriptions of the material recovered from the Roswell crash site.
- The theory satisfies an inclination to tie all the UFO aspects together.
- While resistance to such theories satisfies another inclination, it is difficult to explain the Maury Island story as an elaborate hoax, particularly one that intertwines with conspiracies 20 and 40 years later. The hoax would have had to have been perpetuated by a large number of people with an advanced knowledge of UFOlogy. Common sense prevails against this.
- For the conspiracy theorist this is an ironic point. The same argument—that too many people would have known too much and not said anything for too long—is often used to argue against conspiracy theories.

Cattle mutilations

Despite tons of physical evidence collected over the years, cattle mutilations remain among history's great unsolved serial crimes. Who is reponsible for these ghastly occurrences? Could there be a conspiracy behind this perplexing phenomenon?

Right: Aftermath of an attack on cattle.

Since 1967 and the world-famous mutilation of Snippy the horse (see page 149), witnesses have reported thousands of mysteriously slain livestock: cows with their eyes gouged out and their flesh cut to the bone, their carcasses grossly mutilated. Most reports come from North and South America, but many also have been filed in Australia, Europe, the Caribbean, and Africa.

Hi-tech incisions

Most of the animal carcasses exhibit similar hyper-technical disfigurements. Ranchers have found various soft-tissue organs expertly removed with no clues at the scene as to who, or what, was responsible and why certain beasts are chosen over others. Yet laboratory results showing "cooked hemoglobin" and precision-cut hide and flesh suggest that the animals are the target of an intelligent force.

In "classic" cattle mutilation cases, the animal turns up missing a combination of soft-tissue organs: an eye, an ear, the reproductive organs or udders, or the tight flesh around the mandible, or the tongue cut out deep in the throat. Sometimes patches of hide and, occasionally, internal organs and fetuses are removed. Variations abound, and many of the animals also appear drained of blood and fluids. In some rare cases incisions appear burned as if they had been cut by a laser, or exhibit serrated "cookie-cutter" marks as if cut by precision pinking shears.

Initially, during the early 1970s, a clustering of cases occurred in the upper midwestern United States, in Minnesota, Wisconsin, Kansas, and Oklahoma. The media suggested the deaths might have been the work of bloodthirsty occultists or pranksters, yet many of the wounds appeared surgically precise—the work of experts. The shadow of conspiracy widened as the number of cases rose ominously and spread to 32 states. Conspiracy theories quickly began to take shape.

> "Long-time mutilation researcher Thomas R. Adams ultimately compiled a list of over 250 helicopter sightings around mutilation areas of the time."

Was the military involved?

Black helicopters began to arrive. Area ranchers began reporting a constant stream of unidentified helicopter sightings around the U.S. mutilation sites. Long-time mutilation researcher Thomas R. Adams ultimately compiled a list of over 250 helicopter sightings around mutilation areas of the time. Law enforcement officials eventually came to suspect government involvement. After investigating over a hundred cases in Alabama, Ted Oliphant, the police chief of Fyffe, Alabama, concluded, "In recent mutilation cases—Alabama, 1993 and 1994; California, 1996; and Florida, 1997—pharmaceuticals have been found in bovine blood. They are barbiturates, anti-coagulants, synthetic amphetamines, aluminium-titanium-oxygen-silicon flakes, and antimony . . . According to recent police reports, some investigating officers have claimed that the concentrations of drugs found are not of a veterinary nature, but are pharmaceutical concentrations . . . associated with humans. Among those law enforcement agents who have thoroughly investigated these bovine excision sites, there is a consensus that some kind of medical testing is going on. The additional presence of helicopters on scene, before and after cattle are found dead missing specific organs, leads both victimized

POINTS TO PONDER: SNIPPY THE HORSE

- Found in September 1967 on the King Ranch in the San Luis Valley, Colorado, Snippy the horse was the first widely publicized unusual animal death. She was found missing all her tissue, hide, and hair, from the shoulders to the tip of her nose. Her bones looked polished "like they'd been in the sun for 30 years."
- Snippy's death occurred at the height of a UFO flap, and the owner insisted: "Flying saucers killed my horse!"
- Conservative estimates have it that over 10,000 livestock mutilation cases have occurred in the United States since the first internationally publicized case.

farmers and investigating officers to conclude that there is a connection."

Although rewards have been offered for the arrest and conviction of the perpetrators, no one has ever been charged or convicted, after 40 years and thousands of unsolved cases, of a single act of cattle mutilation. Skeptics insist that the cows simply suffered mundane deaths and disfigurements as a result of predator action or scavenging by coyotes and birds, but none of that explains the black helicopters or the suspicious concentrations of pharmaceuticals.

"After 40 years and thousands of unsolved cases, no one has ever been charged or convicted of a single case of cattle mutilation."

Links to prion-disease sampling

In the early 1980s, livestock mutilation reports officially began to subside even as researchers proposed new theories as to who was responsible. In 1979 pioneering investigator David Perkins had noticed that areas of high incidence appeared downwind and downstream from nuclear power plants, atomic weapons labs, and other facilities for processing uranium. At the time he suspected

Below: Investigators examine a decayed, mutilated carcass found in Colorado.

that many mutilations may have involved environmental monitoring by unknown but well-equipped groups utilizing high-technology. Although only accounting for a small percentage of cases, the theory regained traction during the 1990s even among mainstream scientists.

The 1967 Snippy case appeared at the same time as the spread of the prion- or infectious protein-related, chronic wasting disease known as transmissible spongiform encephalopathy (TSE) or, more coloquially, mad cow disease. Mad cow affects mammalian nervous systems and brains through the development of small cortex depressions. This causes damage to and loss of brain-regulated functions such as memory, personality, and mobility. In humans it is known as Creutzfeldt-Jakob disease.

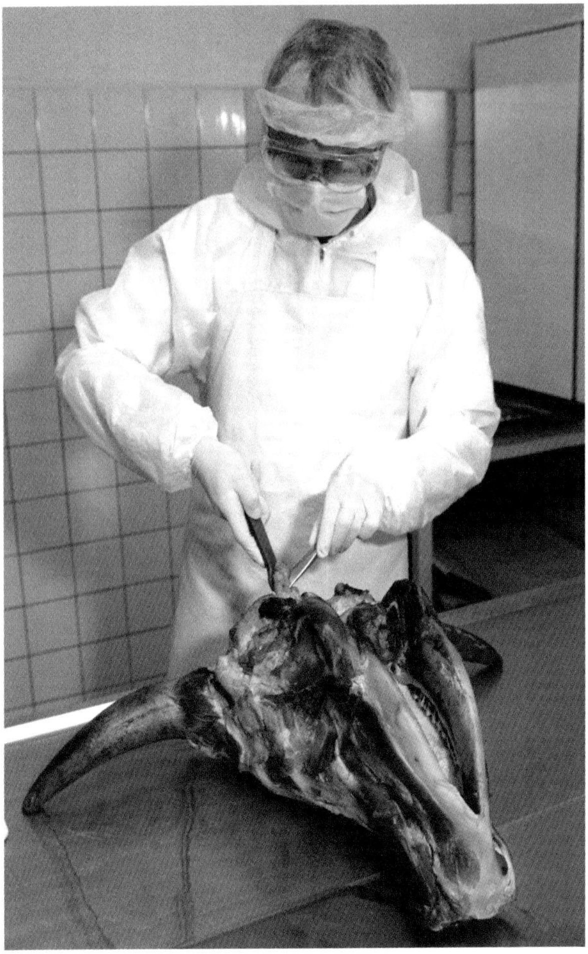

Above: A researcher removes the brain from a cow's skull prior to prion-testing for mad cow disease in 2001.

In 1994 the National Institute of Discovery Sciences (NIDS) began several scientific studies of mutilation cases and reached a landmark conclusion in its position paper of 2003, "Unexplained Cattle Deaths and the Emergence of a Transmissible Spongiform Encephalopathy (TSE) Epidemic in North America":

"Overall, the evidence suggests that animal mutilations are a long-term, covert, prion-disease sampling operation by unknown perpetrators who are aware of a substantial contamination of the beef and venison food supply. Although this paper presents evidence in favor of a motive for animal mutilations, there is still insufficient evidence to identify the perpetrators."

Still, the question of the cattle mutations has never been fully answered. Official U.S. reports suddenly ceased in 1998, and the mystery cattle surgeons appeared to focus their attentions on South American cattle herds. Since the turn of this century, more than 2000 cases have been officially reported in Argentina alone. Among them are cases that continue to defy scientific scrutiny, and which cannot be explained by the prion-disease theory. Some cattle have been found with brains missing but with no break into their cranium; others have been found missing all the copper from their blood. One cow was found with its udder perfectly packed with sand.

In general, however, reported cases of cattle mutilations dropped off considerably after 2002—perhaps the aliens had had their fill of the critters. Mankind's relationship to the animal world has always had an attendant paranoia, based, if nothing else, on the capacity one has to consume the other. In light of the growing corporatization of our food supply today, however, one underlying cause of the cattle mutilations may have less to do with a fear of the animal kingdom or even a fear of aliens. This confounding phenomenon may involve plots by transnational corporate agribusiness concerns ruthlessly trying to accommodate or otherwise manipulate the food supply of an over-populated earth.

Opposite: Entrance to NORAD, the U.S. military's most secure underground military facility, inside Cheyenne Mountain Complex. In 1975, an animal mutilation occurred within sight of the entrance.

PEOPLE IN PURSUIT:

Christopher O'Brien

In 1989, after more than a decade working in New York City as a professional designer, musician, actor, and model, Christopher O'Brien took on a new mission. He moved to the Crestone-Baca region of the San Luis Valley, in south-central Colorado, a desert area regarded as sacred by local inhabitants. He knew of the place because of the famed 1967 case of Snippy the mutilated horse and had only stopped in the valley for a visit. Instead, he remained for nine years and came to learn why the valley holds such fascination to its inhabitants.

O'Brien soon discovered that a UFO light show pulsed and criss-crossed the sky nightly in the valley. He heard, too, strange, rumbling noises coming from beneath the valley, and learned of strands of some weird folklore concerning the recovery of a mysterious crystal skull. Most mysterious of all, however, were the scores of bloodless, mutilated cattle that had been found by residents over the years. O'Brien was so curious about the episodes that he undertook a private investigation, which culminated in the publication of his first book, a popular paperback entitled *The Mysterious Valley*. By the time of its sequel, *Enter the Valley*, O'Brien had become quite an expert on UFO reports, unusual animal deaths, Native American legends, cryptozoology, secret military activity, and the folklore of the San Luis Valley.

Over the years O'Brien has conducted hundreds of interviews and has attempted to verify all of the cattle mutilation accounts he has come across, complete with related UFO sightings. In one instance he investigated telephone calls from nearby NORAD, the U.S. military's secure underground facility, to the Rio Grande sheriff's office discussing mysterious heat-blooms and UFOs that flew into the valley. While he tolerates the theory of extraterrestrial cattle abduction, his personal suspicions are oriented

toward terrestrial conspiracy. "There's quite a bit of evidence to suggest that the military is involved," he notes. "We have well over 250 documented cases of military-style helicopters buzzing around mutilation sights either before, during, or after. A UFO sighting during one of these experiments is pretty rare. However, there are quite a number of reports of helicopters, especially afterward, checking particular sites or areas out. And that would be an indication to me that if it is not the military, then they sure have an interest in it."

Today, as a public speaker, Christopher O'Brien presents his experiences and ideas in the light of regional indigenous cultural life in the valley. He often lectures on the connections between Meso-American ritualized sacrifice and modern-day blood-based paranormal phenomena such as the cattle mutilations. "The gradual progression from ritualized Toltec blood-sacrifice and noble-class self-mutilation to the sobering Aztec practice of human sacrifice," O'Brien claims, "says a great deal about the lengths to which human societies will go to develop an industrialized protein source for the masses." Does a link exist between this and the modern cattle mutilation phenomenon? The questions O'Brien raises are intriguing.

UFO disinformation

In the late 1970s, physicist Paul Bennewitz thought he had discovered a plan for alien domination of the Earth. Was he deliberately misled by government agencies in his search for evidence? Had he come across genuine information that they did not want revealed?

Right: Classic flying saucer model, built by enthusiasts in the 1950s.

Electrical physicist Paul Bennewitz was president of his own company, Thunder Scientific Labs, located in Albuquerque, New Mexico. For many years, he had harbored a keen interest in UFOs. Encouraged by deliberate misinformation from the U.S. military, he became so convinced that he had uncovered something shocking and dastardly that it resulted in his being committed to a mental institute in 1988.

Threats of an alien invasion

Bennewitz thought he had discovered a plan for alien domination of the Earth, and he issued a report about it called "Project Beta." Although various government agencies had received and dismissed such reports for many decades, agents of the Air Force Office of Special Investigations (AFOSI) and the National Security Agency (NSA) realized, this time, that Bennewitz had stumbled onto something that they would rather keep a secret. They decided to use his obsession with UFOs to their advantage.

What Bennewitz had seen, around 1979, was a series of animated lights darting around the wilds of Kirtland Air Force Base in Albuquerque, New Mexico. The lights hovered around the Manzano weapons storage complex at Kirtland, possibly the largest underground repository of nuclear weapons components in the Western world at the time. Located on a small mountain range honeycombed with tunnels and shafts, the military complex was filled with nuclear weapons and replacement parts for all sorts of atomic devices. In early 1980, Bennewitz took pictures of and recorded on 8mm film what he saw, and taped the strange signals that he detected coming from the base. As he listened in to the signals and continued to watch the enigmatic lights, Bennewitz convinced himself that extraterrestrials had an interest in the Earth's military establishments.

It had no small impact on Bennewitz that, during the same period, people were discovering dead and mutilated animals almost weekly around the nearby hamlet of Dulce, New Mexico (see page 148). It was Bennewitz who triggered the movement that transformed this remote outpost into a nexus for UFO spotters for the next two decades. He began to suspect that Dulce harbored an underground alien base, and that the extraterrestrials intended to disarm or cripple the power structure of the U.S. military, the American government, and ultimately, the world. He believed the aliens were using Dulce as a central location from which to conduct reconnaissance, abduct and implant human victims, and perform cattle mutilations.

A victim of military deception

Having compiled detailed notes on what he had seen and recorded, Bennewitz called Kirtland Air Force Base in late 1980 and asked AFOSI agent Richard Doty if he could come to the base and discuss his research. His request was accepted: having been aware of Bennewitz's interest in the base for some time, the AFOSI were keen to establish whether he had been heard something he should not have. As early as July of that year, the AFOSI had employed UFOlogist William Moore to follow Bennewitz and record his activities. If he had stumbled onto something important, there could be a security issue at stake. Bennewitz was a trained scientific professional who had proved himself to be more than competent in his electronics work, and his opinion carried some weight in the right circles.

It turned out that, among the various projects he investigated, Bennewitz had unwittingly stumbled upon powerful ground-based telescopes that the U.S. military used to track Soviet spy satellites. Bennewitz pointed his instruments right at the facility housing these telescopes, but did not have the slightest idea of what he was pointing at. However, the Cold War was far from over and the AFOSI could not take the risk that he might find out.

Below: NSA dishes, monitoring electronic transmissions around the world as part of the United States intelligence network.

PEOPLE IN PURSUIT:

William Moore

Moore had a dubious relationship with the AFOSI, rendering services in exchange for secret UFO-related information. At the Mutual UFO Network (MUFON) convention held in Las Vegas in July 1989, he made a speech that had to be stopped several times to restore order. Trying to explain his role in the Bennewitz case and others like it, he said he had deliberately withheld information from certain researchers, and had reported on their thinking and activities to his contacts in the intelligence world. He had visited Paul Bennewitz on at least four occasions, he said, talked to him many times, and reported on what he found to these same people. He had withheld and blacked out certain parts of UFO-related government documents. He had even passed a deliberately misleading document on to Bennewitz. Moore was warning other researchers that this could happen to them, and indeed already had. And he was promoting a new way to study and research UFOs, a way of accessing tightly held government secrets on UFO activity without getting burned in the process. Moore's approach was to go public after years of maintaining behind-the-scenes contacts with the same kind of military personnel who manipulated and perhaps drove mad the hapless Paul Bennewitz by way of his private obsessions.

Opposite: Kirtland Air Force Base, Albuquerque, New Mexico.

Opposite: A model of a flying saucer, circa 1955.

Following his meeting at Kirtland Air Force base on November 10, 1980, Bennewitz was informed that several officers were "very interested" in his photos, films, and recordings. He was encouraged to continue his research. Bennewitz set himself the task of figuring out the strange transmissions, and found, in a few months, that he had the beginnings of a pattern. The messages read like a science-fiction nightmare, and confirmed his worst fears. The AFOSI provided him with "decoding software," which was specifically tailored to lead him further into the maze of an alien invasion.

Caught up in his own invasion theories, Paul Bennewitz readily accepted the "important information" passed to him by various Air Force officials, and which proved so vital to his research. At their instigation (and his expense), a catalogue of wild stories would become legendary in the history of UFO lore. What started as a small-scale deception of one man went on to spawn a generation of rumors that became widely accepted as true: that aliens had underground bases in the desert; that aliens worked with the government to exchange technology for abduction rights; that aliens farmed human body parts for supper. And so it went on.

In late spring 1981, the AFOSI began to draw Bennewitz's attention away from the base. Doty invited Bennewitz to board a helicopter for a private tour of the Archuleta Mesa near Dulce. Pointing out a number of almost impossibly inaccessible areas that had been carefully planted with old jeeps and storage buildings, Doty told Bennewitz that alien activity was suspected in this area. As long as the lies fitted his theories and hunches, Bennewitz believed them. And as long as his questions kept him away from the sensitive projects underway at Kirtland, the agencies monitoring his activities felt they had done their job of protecting national security. Bennewitz finally cracked in August 1988. No longer able to function, he was committed to a mental facility by his family.

Mind control

Is television a mind-control device put in place to enthrall an unsuspecting audience into passive acceptance of a global consumer culture? Could the possibilities of mind control play a more sinister role in the modern world?

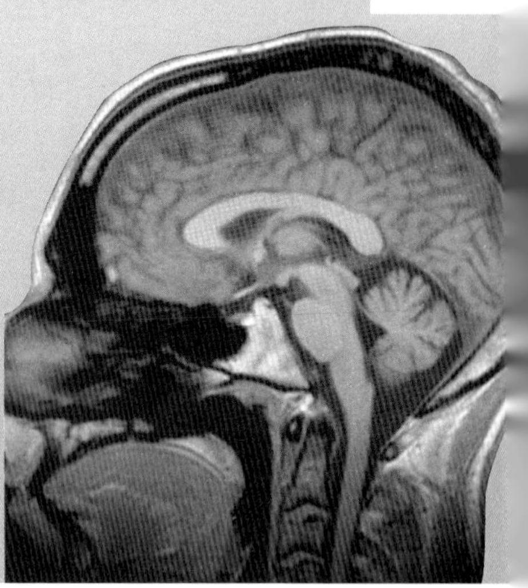

Right: MRI scan showing a sagittal transection through the human brain.

The proposition of such a possibility is evidenced by the recurring theme of mind control in books and movies. Take, for example, the 2004 remake of *The Manchurian Candidate* (based on Richard Condon's 1959 novel), in which transnational corporatism replaces international Communism, the subject of the original 1962 film. The "baddies" in John Frankenheimer's 1962 adaptation were in fact Manchurian; in the 2004 version they had become the executives of Manchurian Global, a corporation with less public face than U.S. Vice President Dick Cheney's corporations, Haliburton and Carlisle. The mind-control technology featured in the 1962 film version had the brainwashed assassin responding to deep hypnosis; the newer movie used microchip implants to achieve control.

Mind manipulation and the assassination of John F. Kennedy

The earliest rumors of mind manipulation arose shortly after JFK's assassination in 1963, with the suggestion that Lee Harvey Oswald had been implanted with a device under the guise of an adenoid operation while living in the Soviet Union. The technology, known as RHIC/EDOM (Radio Hypnotic Intracerebral Control of the brain and Electronic Dissolution of Memory), guided Oswald's actions on November 22, 1963, claims Lincoln Lawrence in his book, *Were We Controlled*.

Oswald certainly had some familiarity with mind alteration. In the summer of 1962, he visited New Orleans assistant district attorney Edward Gillen to ask if LSD was legal, and made several references to Aldous Huxley's *Brave New World*, a classic of psychedelic literature. At the time, the CIA served as one of only a few suppliers of the drug, experimenting with it on soldiers at the Atsugi Naval Base in Japan, where Oswald had been stationed. Did Oswald have a genuine curiosity about LSD, or was this a way he could appear as a mentally unstable Communist sympathizer to a public official? Such a profile was, according to some, what Oswald had been told by his handlers to cultivate.

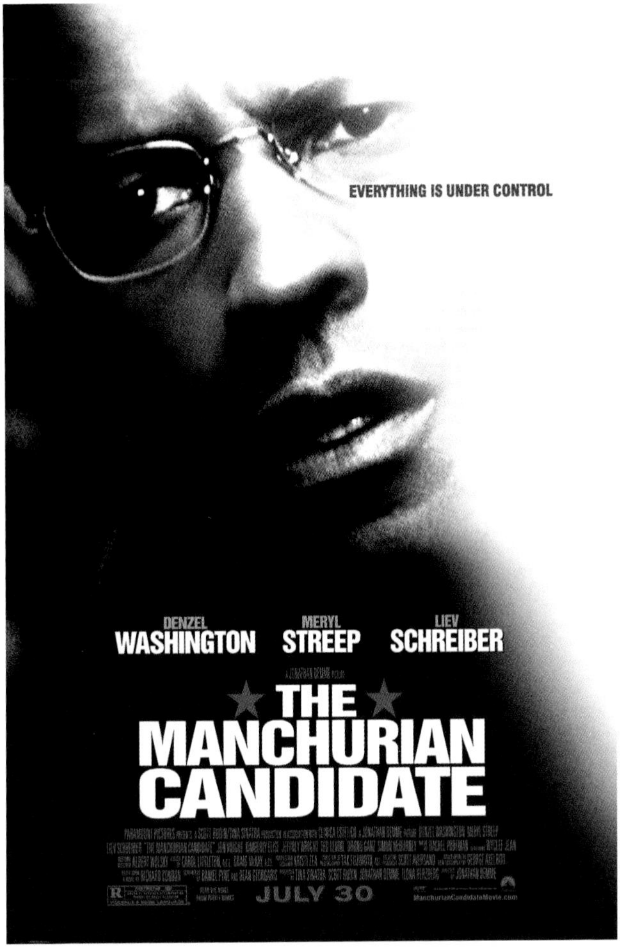

Above: Film poster for *The Manchurian Candidate*, 2004.

Oswald's own assassin, Jack Ruby, also had a connection to psychedelic mind control. In 1964, psychiatrist Louis Joylon West visited Ruby in jail and diagnosed him as paranoid. It was West who had previously downed an elephant by giving it a heavy dose of LSD as part of an experiment at the University of Oklahoma, where he was head of psychiatry. West had also helped plan a rehabilitation program for "pre-delinquent" children that involved administering drugs, lobotomies, and chemical castration, a project later halted by state authorities. In later years, West continued to be involved in other criminal cases that seized the public's attention. He was a psychiatric consultant in the prosecution of Timothy McVeigh, the man ultimately convicted of bombing the Alfred P. Murrah Federal building in Oklahoma City in 1995.

McVeigh, in turn, had told his friend Phil Morawski that the Army had implanted a microchip in his buttock for tracking purposes and for mind control. At one point McVeigh worked for Burns International Security Service's Calspan operation in Buffalo, New York, which included electronic telemetric devices—injectable transponders often used to track pets—among its many products.

PEOPLE IN PURSUIT:

Frank H. Schwable

The most notoriously covert mind control program of the United States' government is the one code-named MKULTRA. (Incidentally, when the manufacturers of a hypnotically violent video game, *Mortal Kombat*, developed a new version, they named it *Mortal Kombat Ultra*, thereby allowing its abbreviation: MKULTRA.)

CIA Director Allen Dulles began MKULTRA in April 1953 but historians find it difficult to document the full extent of the program because succeeding CIA Director Richard Helms destroyed all its records in 1972, in anticipation of Congressional hearings on MKULTRA in the mid-1970s. The program involved a wide variety of processes to develop a mind control weapon, from LSD and other psychedelic drugs (many 1960s counterculture figures such as Timothy Leary served as early volunteers), to electric stimulation, radiation, and sensory deprivation, and it became apparent that many unwitting U.S. citizens had been experimented upon.

How did the United States become involved in such a program? Part of the answer may be found in its pursuit of biowarfare, and in the experiences of Colonel Frank H. Schwable, a former Chief of Staff of the U.S. First Marine Aircraft Wing.

Schwable piloted an American airplane that was shot down and captured on July 8, 1952, during the Korean War. Schwable confessed to a role in a bacteriological warfare project that utilized populations of germ-infested insects dropped onto the enemy. Had Schwable not affirmed them, the accusations by the North Koreans of such a wild story would have held no credibility on the world stage. However, in February 1953, North Korea's Hsinhua News Agency made public Schwable's confession, quoting the following: "The general plan for bacteriological warfare in Korea was directed by the United States' Joint Chiefs of Staff in October 1951. In that month, the Joint Chiefs of Staff sent a directive by hand to the Commanding General, Far East Command (at that time General Ridgway), directing the initiation of bacteriological warfare in Korea on an initially small, experimental stage but expanding in proportions.

The basic objective was at the time to test, under field conditions, the various elements of bacteriological warfare, and to possibly expand the field tests, at a later date, into an element of the regular combat operations, depending on the results obtained and the situation in Korea. The effectiveness of the different diseases available was to be tested, especially for their spreading or epidemic qualities under various circumstances, and to test whether each disease caused a serious disruption to enemy operations and civilian routine or just minor inconveniences, or was contained completely, causing no difficulties. Various types of armament or containers were to be tried out under field conditions and various types of aircraft were to be used to test their suitability as bacteriological bomb vehicles."

The Koreans accompanied the statement with photographs of various recovered bombs including those of the unusual payload, the disease-carrying bugs. Despite the detail provided by Schwable, the official American response was that the story was as false as it was bizarre. The official position in covert intelligence was that the Koreans, as proxies of the Soviets and the Chinese, had brainwashed Schwable into his confession using mind control techniques. This was the moment that the CIA became interested in the subject.

Allen Dulles began MKULTRA two months after Schwable's confession, in order to develop for use by the West the mind control techniques apparently perfectly effected by the Soviets and the Chinese.

Had Schwable been brainwashed? Investigations by the International Red Cross and the World Health Organization of what happened to the American airman never materialized. A 1952 scientific commission, which had among its members witnesses to World War II Japanese germ warfare–specifically, a bacteriological unit run by Shiro Ishii and known as Unit 731–concluded that the charges about the bacteriological bug bombs were true. A preliminary military investigation after the war came to no conclusion.

Most Americans accepted that Schwable had been tortured or brainwashed because they believed the U.S. would never be involved in potentially genocidal bacteriological warfare. Even Schwable himself said: "None of us believes that bacteriological warfare has any place in war since of all the weapons devised, bacteriological bombs alone have as their primary objective casualties among masses of civilians and that is utterly wrong in anybody's conscience."

The United States had, however, employed Nazi and Japanese germ-warfare specialists after World War II. The USA even helped develop Sarin nerve gas, the chemical weapon of choice of the Aum Shinrikyo cult in terror attacks on the Japanese subway system in March 1995. Today, Sarin is among the many bacteriological agents most feared as potential terrorist weapons. Post-9/11, the United States has increased its spending on "biodefense," to study these weapons just as MKULTRA once studied mind control. And this, despite the suspicion of many that the origin of one such agent, anthrax, is a U.S. military laboratory, and that the person responsible for its dispersion in mailings during October 2001 may have worked for the U.S. National Institute of Health.

Below: Marine Corps Officer Col. Frank S. Schwable, pictured after his release from a North Korean prison camp.

Mind control in popular culture

Frank Sinatra, who played Major Bennett Marco in the original movie *The Manchurian Candidate*, found some resistance to its continued release after he acquired the rights. The film was shown only four times on television between 1965 and 1975, and was not re-released in theaters until 1988. During that decade it was difficult to find a copy of the movie in America, a task well-nigh impossible in Eastern European countries, where it was censored, until the collapse of the Soviet Union in 1993. It is perhaps a testament to the extent to which its ideas about mind control had penetrated the consciousness of the American audience.

A familiar theme in movies that expose conspiracies is that in the end the hero becomes de-brainwashed, sheds his crazy conspiracy notions, and is brought in from the cold by secret government agents. The surveillance video that is seen in *The Manchurian Candidate* is similar to a video released shortly after the U.S. government's 9/11 Commission. In this video, the 9/11 hijackers are seen going through airport security. But is that really what is on the tape?

What might reverberate with movie audiences is the similarity in names between the *Manchurian Candidate* character Bennett Marco and Washington DC sniper Lee Boyd Malvo, who was arrested in 2002 in connection with the Beltway sniper attacks. It's not the first coincidence with names from *The Manchurian Candidate*. The original production listed a Janet Leigh and a Laurence Harvey but was missing an Oswald.

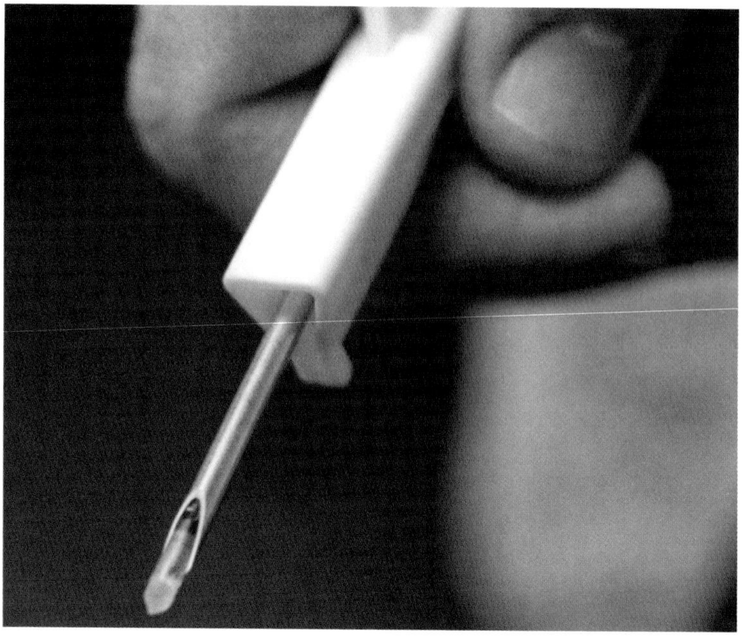

Right: A type of microchip that can be inserted into pets for tracking and identification.

If the movie's hero, Major Marco, had been corrupted by maintaining a conspiracy, not so Captain America, in whose eponymous comic books emerge mind-control themes. Created by Jack Kirby, a legendary figure in the American comic-book industry, the good captain fought Nazis during World War II. In 2004, Marvel Comics released *Captain America and the Falcon: Madbomb*, a reprint collection of some of Kirby's 1976 comic books. Like *The Manchurian Candidate*, *Madbomb* involves a mind-control weapon. However, *Madbomb* more accurately reflects the emerging paranoia of people who felt they had received directed microwaves that were designed to destroy their minds. After the tumultuous politics of the previous decade, many citizens felt they could be going crazy and began attributing this to the development of new technology. In *Madbomb*, Kirby imagined this technology to be a weapon of mass destruction, and alluded to conspiracy theories involving "Men in Black" and underground bunkers, remarkably predating the 1980s stories of Area 51. Kirby even includes in his tale a conspiracy master named Henry Kissinger.

"*Madbomb* more accurately reflects the emerging paranoia of people who felt they had received directed microwaves that were designed to destroy their minds."

"Conspiracy as usual"

The idea of mind control has been called "conspiracy as usual" in that it was simply a standard, if exploitative, business practice. Mind control, however, is a rather unusual way of conducting conspiracy, one that was exposed by two U.S. congressional committees: the Nelson Rockefeller and Senator Frank Church committees of 1975. In the process of revealing various CIA involvements in foreign assassinations and domestic surveillance, these government bodies released evidence from public files that proved such CIA brainwashing programs as MKULTRA did in fact exist and could no longer be regarded as the province of crazy conspiracy theorists. Thus exposed, the programs had to be abandoned—some say forced underground—and a great reform of the intelligence world ensued. Today some critics believe that the reform process weakened the CIA to the point that it was kept from preventing 9/11.

Moon landings

One of the most watched events in human history, the Moon landing on July 20, 1969, represented the pinnacle of human technological achievement. But, as some skeptics would argue with the support of millions around the world, was this great moment in human history actually one of the most masterly hoaxes of all time?

Right: NASA image of the Moon.

Opinion polls, such as a 1999 Gallup poll, show that up to six percent of the American public doubt that man ever landed on the Moon, instead suspecting that the U.S. government concocted one of the most elaborate and audacious schemes imaginable, firing empty rockets into the sky and filming the astronauts on a secret set to counterfeit the momentous events. The government then did it five more times over the next three years, disbelievers claim. What's more, Moon-landing skepticism is current all over the world.

Hatching the world's greatest hoax

Among the leading proponents of the claim that the Moon landings—or, at the very least, aspects of them—were faked are Bill Kaysing, author of *We Never Went to the Moon: America's Thirty Billion Dollar Swindle!*, and photographer David Percy, author of *Whistle-Blowers*, which looks in particular detail at supposed clues left in moon-landing pictures by whistle-blowing technicians looking to tip off the public. Their arguments cover motive, means and execution, and they claim the proof is visible to anyone with eyes to see.

"The space race had become a potent weapon in the Cold War propaganda battle, and the USA was losing."

In 1957 the USSR successfully launched into orbit Sputnik, the first artificial satellite, and followed this up with a series of other firsts—first dog in space, first man in space, first space walk, and first lunar probe. The space race had become a potent weapon in the

Cold War propaganda battle, and the USA was losing both the race and the battle. Accordingly, in 1962, President Kennedy gave the famous speech in which he set forth an incredibly ambitious goal: that within the decade the United States would land men on the Moon and bring them back. Moon-shot sceptics argue that Kennedy and NASA knew even then that this was an impossible dream: it was simply too expensive and too far beyond the nation's scientific and technological capabilities, plus, crucially, levels of radiation and energetic particles in space, away from the protective shield of the Earth's magnetic field, would quickly prove lethal to astronauts. NASA colluded with this gargantuan fraud to secure massive long-term funding.

Faking the Moon

There are various versions of how the hoax was executed. Kaysing's is among the most elaborate and entertaining. He claims that while global attention was fixed on an empty Saturn V rocket that blasted off from Florida, only to fall back to Earth and ditch into the remote polar seas, the real action was taking place at a secret base in Nevada. The astronauts, some of whom had been brainwashed using

Below: Laika, the first dog sent into space by the USSR, in November 1957.

"*Manchurian Candidate*" methods, were spirited off to Las Vegas where the Mafia, in on the plot, entertained them with booze and showgirls until it was time for them get to work on huge fake lunar sets, constructed in underground caverns with help from Hollywood specialists. Here an array of special effects was used to film fake TV footage of the landing and the moon walks, and to generate the hundreds of photos later circulated as "proof" that the impossible had been achieved. When it was time for the astronauts to "return to Earth" they were flown to a secret base in the Pacific, packed into a dummy space capsule, and dropped into the sea from an airplane. All the other aspects of the mission were also faked, down to the moon rock supposedly brought back by the "astronauts."

Blowing the whistle

Astonishingly, given the titanic scale of this insidious intrigue, there were no leaks and no slip-ups. Presumably the KGB and other enemy intelligence agencies would have scrutinized the project in minute detail, yet even they were unable to uncover any "smoking guns." But where the professionals failed, amateurs have succeeded. In particular, many photographers were initially skeptical at the quality of the pictures returned by the astronauts, who would have had to overcome immense obstacles, including using essentially ordinary cameras to expose delicate film in a vacuum, in extreme temperatures and despite a barrage of cosmic radiation. The cameras used had no viewfinders and no light meters and the astronauts had to operate them while wearing thick bulky gloves.

"Perhaps most tellingly, there are no stars visible in any of the photos, although with no atmosphere the stars should have been gloriously visible."

When they looked closer at the photographs, they identified a host of apparent howlers. The skeptics contend that with no atmosphere on the Moon the light conditions should have been ones of high contrast, with a single light source and no scattering of light to help "fill in" (i.e. lighten) shaded surfaces and shadows. Yet the photos clearly show lots of filling-in and softened shadows, not to mention such giveaways as non-parallel shadows and shadows of differing lengths—all evidence of multiple light sources (i.e. studio lights) close to the set, which can even be seen reflecting off surfaces such as visors in some shots. Perhaps most tellingly, there are no stars visible in any of the photos, although with no atmosphere the stars should have been gloriously visible. Were these obvious errors introduced by disgruntled technicians, seeking to alert the public without endangering their lives? Other giveaways include the lack of a blast crater underneath the lunar lander and waves in the U.S.

flag planted by the astronauts (which should not be possible in a vacuum, and prove there was a slight breeze during the filming.)

Above: Astronaut Buzz Aldrin walks on the surface of the Moon. July 20, 1969.

Coming back to Earth

While there is not a shred of direct evidence for the lurid claims of Bill Kaysing, the mass of indirect "evidence" from the lunar pictures may appear convincing. However, both NASA and the vast majority of independent scientists and experts who have looked at the issue argue that this so-called evidence is based on simple ignorance of conditions on the lunar surface, together with some embarrassingly basic errors by the photo skeptics about photography and lighting. The crucial plank of the Moon-landing skeptics' argument is that lunar photos show evidence of multiple, close light sources, when there should only be one, extremely distant light source (the Sun.)

James Oberg

PEOPLE IN PURSUIT:

In the battle against the hoax claims, NASA has sometimes been its own worst enemy. In 2002 the agency commissioned respected space writer James Oberg to produce a book that would definitively rebut the hoax theories, but just a few months later they changed their minds and canceled his contract in peremptory fashion. James Oberg is best known today in the USA as NBC's "space consultant," but he has had a long and distinguished history as a NASA expert designing and chronicling missions involving link-ups in space (including the original International Space Station assembly mission), and subsequently as a writer and consultant on the global space industry.

After years of ignoring the moon landing hoax allegations, NASA were finally stung into action by a Fox TV documentary pushing the conspiracy theory in 2001. Oberg, who had already written extensively on the history of the space program and the space race, had been pushing NASA for some years to commission a series of monographs dealing with what he calls the "many different widespread cultural myths about space activities," from astronaut UFO sightings to the Moon-hoax allegations. Goaded by the Fox documentary NASA finally agreed to the latter idea, and Oberg started to gather materials. However, an ABC news report of November 4,

This argument is easily dismissed. Firstly, the Earth seen from the Moon is extremely bright—the full Earth seen from the Moon is 68 times brighter than a full moon on Earth. More importantly, moon rock and moon dust are highly reflective, and this accounts for the filling-in, reflections, and apparent multiple light sources. The nature of photography in such conditions—fast exposures because of strong lighting—meant that the stars, much fainter by comparison with the brightly illuminated surface, were not visible, just as they cannot be seen in similar photos taken during the night on Earth. Non-parallel shadows of varying length are the result of the unevenness of the lunar surface and the effects of perspective in photographs (which are two-dimensional renditions of three-dimensional realities.) Radiation in space is not lethal to astronauts if their exposure is limited, as proved by a range of experiments and trials by many space agencies. No crater is visible because in fact the lunar lander produced relatively gentle thrust, and a hard surface was specifically chosen for the landing site. The cameras used by the astronauts were modified for ease of use and the astronauts had training. And the flag in lunar photos from the first mission had creases because the horizontal rod along the top did not extend completely—in later missions, astronauts deliberately put creases in the flags because they liked the way they looked.

Skeptics also forget that, while there is no hard proof of what would constitute the greatest hoax/conspiracy of all time, there is hard proof that we did go to the Moon. For instance, laser reflectors left on the lunar surface are still used today by Earth-based astronomers to monitor moon-quakes.

Opposite: Buzz Aldrin and the U.S. flag on the Moon. According to conspiracy theorists, the creases on the flag, which should not appear in a vacuum, are proof of the hoax.

2002, characterized the commission derisively as "the space agency spend[ing] a few thousand dollars trying to prove to some people that the United States did indeed land men on the moon." More media criticism followed, suggesting that by specifically rebutting the claims NASA were lending them too much credence, and that they were wasting taxpayers' money pandering to "lunatics." Spooked, the agency paid Oberg for the work he'd done and revoked his contract. Unfortunately, it seems likely that their indecision has simply provided ammunition to those who believe they have something to hide.

"It's not just a few crackpots and their new books and Internet conspiracy sites," Oberg wrote in 1999. "There are entire subcultures within the USA, and substantial cultures around the world, that strongly believe the landing was faked. I'm told that this is official dogma still taught in schools in Cuba–plus wherever else Cuban teachers have been sent, such as Sandanista Nicaragua, and Angola."

Further reading

Chapter 1

Acharya S (1999), *The Christ Conspiracy: The Greatest Story Ever Sold*, Adventures Unlimited Press: Kempton, Illinois

Baigent, M., Leigh, H., and Lincoln, R. (1983), *Holy Blood, Holy Grail*, Dell Publishing Company: New York

Buechner, Howard A. (1988), *Adolf Hitler and the Secrets of the Holy Lance*, Thunderbird Press: Metairie, Louisiana

Dunn, Christopher (1998), *The Giza Power Plant: Technologies of Ancient Egypt*, Bear & Company: Rochester, Vermont

Gardner, Laurence (1997), *Bloodline of the Holy Grail* (Rev Exp ed) Fair Winds Press: Beverly, MA

Knight, C. and Lomas, R. (2001), *The Hiram Key*, Fair Winds Press: Beverly, MA

Muck, Otto (1978), *The Secrets of Atlantis* (Translated by Fred Bradley) New York Times Book: New York

Parfrey, Adam (1991), *Apocalypse Culture*, Feral House: Los Angeles

Phillip, Graham (2004), *The Templars and the Ark of the Covenant*, Bear & Company: Rochester, VT

Russell, Bertrand (1946), *History of Western Philosophy*, Routledge: London

Smith, Jerry E. and Piccard, George (2005), *Secrets of the Holy Lance*, Adventures Unlimited Press: Kempton, Illinois

Sora, Steven, (2004), *The Lost Colony of the Templars*, Destiny Books: Rochester, Vermont

Tabbert, Mark A. (2005), *American Freemasons*, New York University Press: New York

Tabbert, Mark (2006), *American Freemasons: Three Centuries of Building Communities*, New York University Press: New York

Watkins, Larissa P. (2003), *American Masonic Periodicals, 1811–2001. A Bibliography of the Library of the Supreme Council, 33°, S.J.*, Oak Knoll Press: New Castle, DE

Chapter 2

Armstrong, John (2003), *Harvey and Lee*, Quasar: Arlington, Texas

McClellan, Barr, (2003), *Blood, Money and Power: How LBJ killed JFK*, Hannover House: Fayetteville, AR

McCoy, Alfred (1972), *The Politics of Heroin in Southeast Asia*, Harper & Row: New York

Ramsey, Robin (2000), *Conspiracy Theories: Almost Everything you Need to Know in One Essential Guide*, Pocket Essentials: London

Sick, Gary (1991), *October Surprise: America's Hostages in Iran and the Election of Ronald Reagan*, Random House: New York

Thomas, Kenn and Keith, Jim (1996), *The Octopus: Secret Government and the Death of Danny Casolaro*, Feral House: Los Angeles

Turner, William and Christian, John (2006), *The Assassination of Robert F. Kennedy*, Carroll and Graf: New York

Zirbel, Craig (1992), *The Texas Connection*, Warner Books: New York

Chapter 3

Bishop, Greg, (2005), *Project Beta: The Story of Paul Bennewitz, National Security, and the Creation of a Modern UFO Myth*, Paraview Pocket Books: New York

Kaysing, Bill, (1976), *We Never Went to the Moon: America's Thirty Billion Dollar Swindle!* Health Research Books: Pomeroy, WA

Lawrence, Lincoln (1967), Were We Controlled? *The Assassination of President Kennedy*, New Hyde Park University Books, Inc.: New York

Lusar, Rudolf (1960), *German secret weapons of the Second World War*, 2nd ed. Neville Spearman: Walden, Essex

Martin, Jim (2000), *Wilhelm Reich and the Cold War*, Flatland Books: Mendocino, CA

Moore, William (ed.) 1984, *Nazi Flying Saucers*, William L. Moore Publications, Burbank, Calif.

O'Brien, Christopher (1996) , *Mysterious Valley*, St. Martin's Press: New York

Redfern, Nick (2005), *Body Snatchers in the Desert*, Paraview Pocket Books: New York

Roth, Christopher F. (2005), "Ufology as Anthropology: Race, Extraterrestrials, and the Occult" in E.T. *Culture: Anthropology in Outerspaces*, ed. by Debbora Battaglia, Duke University Press: Durham, NC

Steele, E. J., Lindley, R. A., and Blanden, R. V. (2001), *Lamarck's Signature: How Retrogenes Are Changing Darwin's Natural Selection Paradigm*, Basic Books: New York

Steven, Henry (2003), *Hitler's Flying Saucers: A Guide to German Flying Discs of the Second World War*, Adventures Unlimited Press: Kempton, IL

Vallee, Jacques (1980), *Messengers of Deception*, Bantam Books: New York

Vesco, Renato (1967), *Intercept UFO*, Pinnacle Books: New York

Index

Numbers in italics signify image captions.

PICTURE CREDITS

The publishers would like to thank the following for permission to reproduce images.

Corbis p. 41; Dreamstime: p. 24 (top); Getty Images: pp. 26, 67, 69, 70, 74, 75, 82, 85, 88, 90, 95, 103 (top), 105, 106, 107, 108, 112 (both), 113, 137, 139, 153, 156, 157, 158, 163; Mary Evans: pp. 15, 140, 143; NASA: pp. 2, 5, 86, 166, 169, 170; Photolibrary: pp. 22–23; Rex Features: pp. 79, 80; Richard Burgess: p. 83; Topfoto: pp. 6, 19, 24 (bottom), 40 (top), 44, 45, 52 (bottom), 61, 64, 76, 78, 98, 101, 110, 118, 119, 121, 123, 124, 127, 128, 131, 133, 135, 141, 145, 150, 152, 159, 161, 164, 167